I0825452

JAYDRA JOHNSON

NOTES ON
ART & TRASH

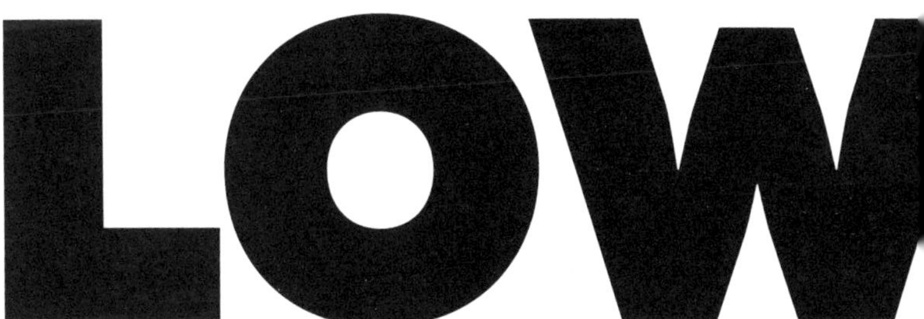

Fonograf Editions
Portland, OR

Cover and text design by Mike Corrao

First Edition, First Printing

FONO33

Published by Fonograf Editions
www.fonografeditions.com

Distributed by NYU Press
NYUPress.org

[clmp]

Fonograf Editions is a proud member of the Community of Literary Magazines and Presses

ISBN: 979-8-9875890-7-6
ISBN (ebook): 978-1-964499-28-4
ISBN (hardcover): 978-1-964499-29-1
LCCN: 2024935598

LOW

NOTES ON ART & TRASH

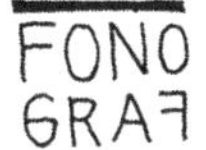

Fonograf Editions

CONTENTS

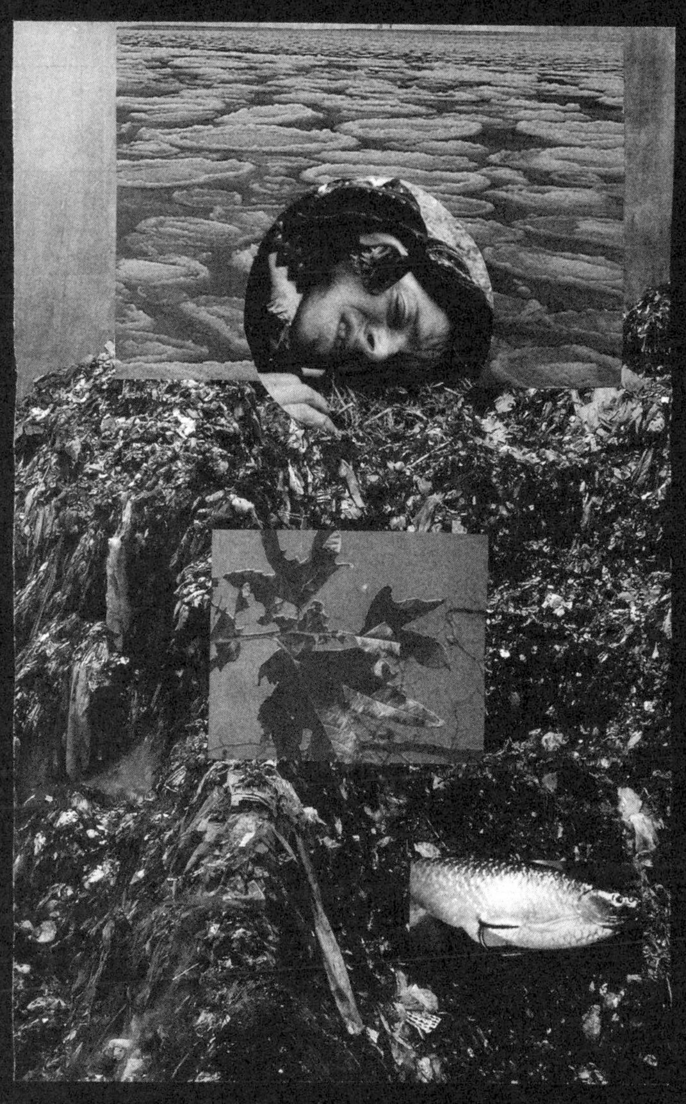

RITUALS TO SEE TRASH #1

1. Approach the podium. Give your name to the lady with the hairnet. Hear her say your account is past due. Consider yourself marked. Try to remember how many days in a row she has said this. Say I am sorry and thank you. Dread telling your mom.

2. Enter the line and take a tray. The tray is beige. The tray is thick, rounded plastic. Later your brother will eat from a plastic tray exactly like this one. He will be in a prison, not a school, but you don't know that yet. He has not yet had to endure the class warfare of cafeteria lunch or the American penal system.

3. Slide your tray along the stainless steel track and let other ladies in hairnets place mounds of things into the tray's compartments. Green beans or peas? Say green beans. Say please and thank you. Feel bad that you are not more grateful. Hate this food. Hate this food so much, but don't show it. It is not the lunch ladies' fault. It is not your parents' fault. Maybe it is your fault. Remember that life isn't fair. Think *life isn't fair* while you walk out from the lunch line room with your horrible food into the cafeteria.

4. Watch your jiggling meat stuff jiggle while you walk. As you pass the trash can, pause and stare into its gray mouth. See the potato smears. See the milk spray. Smell the warm ranch dressing mixed with what has to be cat food gravy.

5. Take your tray to your usual table. Your friend is already sitting down eating carrot sticks and perfect, purple grapes from tiny Tupperware containers. Bite into your roll, unbuttered, sweaty from the steam

table. Eat your mushy green beans. Eat your salted apple slices, their bitter rinds.

6. Look askance at the other kids. Try not to stare. Try not to see the Lunchables, the homemade sandwiches, the all-natural strawberry yogurt cups. Smell Doritos. Salivate. Turn back to your tray. Stick your fork into the ice cream scoop of instant mashed potatoes. Pick the gristle from your turkey gravy—a gelatin ooze flecked with brown animal tissue.

7. Catch sight of another school lunch kid, his home-cut hair grown out in uniform length. He looks like a lost animal. Stare at his thin, spiky hair. Stare at his shoes. Swear you can see them crumbling before you, the rubber flaking away from the canvas like the paint peeling from his house. The boy is on your bus route. Sometimes you talk on the ride to school in the morning, but mostly you smell his coat over the mustiness of the bus seats and try to guess from the stench which drugs the people in his house are doing.

8. Chew your gruel and avert your eyes. Taste the salty nothingness of this carbohydrate science project. Talk to your friend about her dance competition, about church, about top ten radio hits.

9. Look at your tray and think pig. Think dog. Think feed. Spear a soggy green bean on your flimsy lunchroom fork. You can't take another bite of the meat goo or you'll barf. Push your tray away and wait for recess to start. Thank god when recess starts.

10. Get up to dump your tray. The mute colors in the garbage can match the puke colors of the tiles, the walls, and the wood laminate tables. Feel like an ugly girl in an ugly world full of low-intensity suffering. Sense that this is only the beginning of a life where you will get, pretty much, the worst of everything. For a few seconds, watch the other kids swing their colorful, insulated lunch boxes onto their confident shoulders. See them moving like angels, almost floating, out to recess.

11. Slam your tray against the garbage can's lip. For four seconds, let yourself feel pissed. I mean, really fucking angry. Sorry for yourself. Then stop. Feel embarrassed that you're being a brat. Place your fork in the bucket of dirty blue water. Stack your slimy plastic tray on the silver rolling cart with the other plastic trays. Make eye contact with the lunch money lady and smile.

Note: In poetry, a crown is a series of sonnets concerned with a single theme or addressed to one person. Each of the sonnets explores one aspect of the theme, and is linked to the sonnets that come before and after it through repetition: the final line of one sonnet becomes the first line of the next.

I was very young, perhaps seven or eight years old, when I came to understand that I was not just bad, but a special kind of bad. I was trash. And because trash has a habit of gathering, of piling up, of rotting itself, of changing everything it touches into yet more untouchable garbage—unsanitary, unsightly—so was my family, and so were some of my neighbors and classmates and friends. I knew I was trash because I had listened to my teachers and absorbed the culture of *Cops*, shopping malls, MTV, nationally syndicated sitcoms, and the general tenor of the Clinton administration. Evidence that I fulfilled a certain stereotype, at least to some degree, abounded.

We lived within spitting distance of the train tracks. Out my window, I saw trailers and manufactured homes, quads and dirt bikes, late model cars, and a burn pile in the yard. I heard country music, *You Might be a Redneck If*, and a lilting rural drawl. The grown-ups had trouble finding work, and the work they did find hurt their bodies when they did it. Cheap cigarettes and mentholated chew graced every mouth, staining our teeth to match our arms and necks—a dusty brownish red.

What I didn't know then was that I didn't make myself trash, nor did my parents. We were born into its centuries-old inheritance. Trash as a descriptor for people started four hundred years ago in a place I couldn't have expected, but that now doesn't seem that surprising. It started with Shakespeare.

There is blood everywhere in *Othello*: on the battlefields of Cyprus, on the floors and walls of a kill room, on the shimmering blade of a sword. Inside the brothel where he lured them, Iago has secretly stabbed Roderigo to death and mangled Cassio, whose split leg stains the stage an imaginary red. When others discover the carnage, Iago gropes for a plausible scapegoat to blame for his murderous sin. He picks the whore.

"Gentlemen all, I do suspect this trash to be a party in this injury," Iago says, pointing at Bianca, the courtesan. Then, later, about the massacre, "This is the fruits of whoring."

Iago's slander marks the first recorded instance—in the year 1604—of the use of the word trash to describe a person in this way: as low-down, classless, worthless, and of poor character, even criminal. As an epithet, trash both objectifies and denigrates its target. Here, in its first written use, it smears a sex worker.

This fact is hardly scandalizing; the prostitute is a legacy patsy. It's been this way since the beginning. In the Christian Bible's Book of Genesis, Judah learns that his daughter-in-law "played the harlot" and thus became pregnant. "Bring her out and let her be burned!" he says, as in, let her be burned at the stake. In truth, he was the one who had fucked and impregnated her, yet she was the one getting crossed.

Back in the Shakespearean brothel, Bianca maintained her innocence while Iago placed her under arrest. He dragged her off, shackled, as a prop in his own heroic narrative. She went from trash to inmate in minutes, foretelling the future with disturbing accuracy—a future now in which entire trash classes are still blamed, restrained, abused, and jailed. This is how trash started as a lie against a woman, a blame game, a power trip, and an unearned punishment.

o

Trash started as a lie against a woman, but by the time I was born in 1988, the term had become, through centuries of repetition, a kind of cultural truth. Trash had spread across the Atlantic and become a label for all sorts of poor whites, not just the sluts and accused criminals, and lasted long enough to mark my parents as members of the lower classes. My mother, a baby-faced brunette with shockingly good teeth, met my dad, a pro-am dirt bike racer, at the auto parts store where they both worked the cash registers. They got pregnant when my mom was still a teenager, and then they got married. I arrived a few months later, naked and screaming, fantastic and doomed, in the white trash wonderland of Lane County, Oregon.

People fed their chickens and planted potatoes in the neighboring towns and out in the unincorporated country, just a few miles from the hospital where I cried in my little pink hat. They stirred big jugs of Kool Aid and ate ample helpings of gas station biscuits & gravy from paper trays. They raced souped-up trucks, Frankenstein-ed with parts they salvaged from the half-dead machines hunched on their expansive, wild lawns. My white trash neighbors kicked up wake in the murky reservoirs with the motors of their fishing boats, and praised Jesus in the pews of the Baptist church, and after that, they browsed each other's yard sales. Trailer parks hugged the winding highways, and subdivisions of modest, plain houses arranged themselves along the curlicues of cul-de-sacs.

I was born to a long line of working-class people: loggers, maids, cooks, welders, and car salesmen. This lineage also included people who refused or were excluded from work because of disability, school failure, or the compulsion to party. We've been musicians, bikers, and thieves. We've been sex workers. Some of us have even been inmates, forced to work while in shackles. I grew up this way among my trashy brethren—often working, sometimes not, often on welfare, sometimes not, often being punished for our speech or customs or clothes or living arrangements or choices, sometimes not.

It didn't take me long to learn where I stood in the world. All I had to do was pay attention to what was said about people like me and the ways we were treated by schools, churches, bosses, and the law.

o

Although I didn't learn about *Othello* until graduate school, and I didn't learn about Judah at church, I still learned about people like me anytime I paid attention. I listened eagerly during Sunday school, where our story time focused on great men like Noah. While the teachers read aloud a kid-friendly version of his story, we hunched over low tables with coloring pages that glorified his brave, pious journey. I fisted nubby crayons to color in the outlines of Noah's bulging ark, bursting with zebras, elephants, horses, and dogs. Noah was a good man who, like Christ, was a savior. There weren't any women in the picture, as I remember it, though Noah must have had a wife. I assume that when the waters rose, the whores were left on land with the rest of the sinners to fight for their lives, only to succumb to the flood.

When women appeared in the Bible, they were anything but blameless. At Sunday school, I also watched puppet shows in which our teachers depicted the story of the first good man Adam and his irreverent, curious Eve. Like me, Eve craved knowledge and its promise of power. She let the Satanic snake seduce her, almost too easily, with his plush, red apple. At five years old, I had a hard time understanding that any knowledge could be forbidden, so I perfectly understood her decision. I wanted to know everything, and so did she. Eve, I learned from the soft fabric puppets, was the first fallen woman. She was the one who made us sinners. This was the fruit of another kind of whoring.

At home, I saw women reduced to trash, despite their resistance to such treatment. I watched my aunt's boyfriend, enraged over their break-up, throw boxes of her belongings from the window of his car. As the boxes hit the uneven blacktop, their flaps burst open, and their contents—clothing, important papers, dishes, mementos—spilled out While he screamed, "Fuck you, bitch, you whore," he screamed. My aunt and mom cried and cussed back. Then, he sped away, leaving the task of cleaning up the mess to the women. Meanwhile, inside the house, Papa called Nana stupid for overcooking salmon patties and lazy for failing to sweep the floor. "Oh, shut up," she said back, grimacing, but I could tell by the look on her face that it hurt her.

On TV, Al Bundy from *Married... With Children* was one of the few working-class guys I saw on the major networks. Al was a real asshole who objectified, fat-shamed, and blamed the women in his life, including his own wife, the trashy-hot Peggy, a redhead with a bad attitude who hailed from a clan of hillbillies, including a morbidly obese mother, who Al loathed. Al's primary enemy, Marcy, a lazily-written, stereotypical feminist, earned boos from the live studio audience who, conversely, went wild over the gratuitous show of boobs and butts and laughed at Al's sleazy jokes.

On a different channel, cops chased shirtless, drug-addled men—many of them faceless due to privacy pixelations—down gravel driveways or pulled them from cars or coaxed them out of weathered dwellings with scuffed up doors and assorted crap on their stoops. My trashy brethren also graced the stages of daytime talk shows, where the hosts goaded them into making a carnival of their various traumas. I sat cross-legged on the carpet and watched the losers of America perform my life and all its possible misfortunes while my elders worked and cleaned and gardened. Absorbed in the colorful theatrics of our five free television channels, I learned how the world saw people like me—like us—and for what kinds of behavior and self-presentations I might later be shamed.

At Vacation Bible School, a free summer program, I made a refrigerator magnet lion using cut yellow felt and googly eyes. We made the magnets to reinforce the story of Daniel in the lion's den. God saved Daniel, a good boy, because he was found "blameless before Him." There weren't any women in that parable either, whores or otherwise. I brought my lion home and gave it to my mom, who smiled and crowed about my craftsmanship. She placed it high up on the side of the refrigerator filled with bland, government-subsidized food. There, from its place of honor, the lion watched me, waiting to see what kind of girl I'd become.

o

In middle school, I was becoming the kind of girl who would do anything to be accepted by people I thought were good. Money problems and substance abuse among the older members of my household made home increasingly crowded and chaotic, so I spent as much time as possible out of the way, often sleeping over at my Christian friends' houses on weekends. On Sunday mornings, my friends and I sometimes chose to skip the campy, performative atmosphere of youth group, opting instead to sit in on the more somber adult services. From the pulpit, I would watch a clean-cut pastor in an aggressively starched, pastel-hued shirt deliver impassioned sermons about the meek inheriting the Earth, heavenly rewards, and maintaining faith through adversity. Bible verses, often from the Psalms or the books of the apostles, punctuated these ecstatic speeches.

"This poor man cried, and the Lord heard him and saved him out of all his troubles," the pastor read. Flecks of his spit formed a halo in the glow of the stage lighting. God saves the poor, I heard, provided they are good and faithful, which, it seemed obvious to me, my family wasn't. My first clue was this church—god's house—huge and dramatically lit, replete with vaulted ceilings and a baptismal pool. Its immaculateness and glory couldn't have been more different than the houses in which we dwelt.

Shiny, well-tuned instruments adorned the stage, and each was hooked up to a system of mics and speakers that carried pop-inspired worship music into every corner of the space. As I looked around the solid-wood sanctuary filled with well-fed, well-dressed people, I wondered what they had done to show god that they were good and faithful. Why did god give them riches while denying comfort to me and countless others across the globe? I thought about their clean, bright houses, their second refrigerators, and the speedboats parked in their driveways. Meanwhile, many of the houses of my childhood had airy cupboards, cops at the door, or junk cars parked out front.

I tried to be a girl good enough for god to hear my cries, good enough to earn the godly grace that could save my family from the indignity of low wages, debt, charity, and jails. I tried not to want too much. I tried to have faith, to keep my motives pure, but over years and years of prayers and not-sinning, nothing changed. If anything, it got worse. That I was a bad girl from a bad family was the only thing that made sense.

o

I was a bad girl from a bad family, but I tried in every way to prove I was good. Maybe if I did god's good work, I would be rewarded. In the early mornings on school days, I donned a reflective orange vest and carried a yellow flag out to my post at the crosswalk, where I guided my fellow students across the street, fulfilling my duty as a safety patrol member. In the afternoons, I mentored younger students in a reading program. I kept quiet during lessons and accepted what my teachers taught without question. When my classmate Crystal barked at me in the hallways and called me a dog and a dyke, I was too cowardly to retort or shove her into the gray-blue lockers. I was afraid of the punishment I might get from her, the principal, and god. But I wasn't always so good. A year later, when I found out Crystal was hit by a car, an accident that left her seriously injured though alive, I smiled and said she deserved it. This remark earned me the scorn of my best friend's good Christian mother.

In seventh grade, the poorest girl in school who had weepy eyes and stringy hair—a girl whose house was rumored to have holes in the floor where the dirt came through—noticed I wore the same pair of pants every day. I had strategically chosen the stretchy, black flares as my pants for the year when I did my annual school shopping because I had seen the popular girls, the ones with streaky blonde bobs and Abercrombie sweatshirts, wearing them. I knew they would stay in style and stretch to fit my still-growing body, providing my trashiness some cover. When the poorest girl in school confronted me about them, loudly enough for the whole class to hear, I wanted to burn her where she stood, but I couldn't muster a comeback. A few kids snickered and rolled their eyes in pity.

Similarly, when Erica or Michelle, another couple of girls by whom I felt taunted, ridiculed me for wearing Payless shoes and counterfeit Tommy Hilfiger, I didn't draw blood from either of their powdered noses. Instead, I waited until after school, when

I tried to spread rumors about them at sleepovers. I judged them without mercy for every tiny infraction: a wrong answer in math class or a bad hair day or an unfashionable skirt. Sometimes, like Shakespeare's men, I even called them sluts.

But mostly, I sat at my desk and studied my vocabulary words. While I did so, I plotted my revenge—revenge that I imagined would be a life well-lived, somewhere far away from the lumber mills and gas stations of my white trash community. Imagining a lifetime there was hell to me, and I wished it only on my enemies. I dreamed up a future me who would, through focused study and academic excellence, earn public accolades and a shit-ton of money. In this fantastic future, I would be blameless before god and everybody.

My fantasies cut me from the image of my life, from the things and people I loved, and pasted me onto a different background—one populated by people of a certain taste and class. In my effort to succeed, I did not understand that I had already lost because I believed what the world said about poor people like me and our valueless, parasitic existence. At school, I tried to be even better than what I was, unaware that my own aspirations were a form of trash talk that played on a loop in my head all day.

o

Another message that played on a loop in my head was the half-truth that hard work pays off. The right kind of work, I learned from my teachers and parents, could be traded for dollars and degrees. The degrees in question were diplomas, but I also understood them as degrees of separation between my present state and a brighter, whiter ideal. Nobody ever said it this way, but what mattered was whiteness and how good a white one could be. White was a mortgage, a clean criminal record, clean piss, clean clothes, some institutional legitimacy. White was also in grammar, in perfect English with its carefully enunciated g's and its absence of double negatives, perhaps even the King's English with a few Shakespearean flourishes. White was in white-collar work, in poems about horses in white winter fields. White whites—the Shakespeares, George Washingtons, and Ernest Hemingways—received our teachers' attention, and their light outshone the shine that emanated from us students, who dimmed and wilted slowly in our seats. The occasional whitewashed hero of the new classless, raceless America also made appearances—your MLKs, Ghandis, and Iroquois diplomats—to teach a lie about equality and loving one's enemies. People worth attending to were well-educated, pious, and heroic. They were the leaders of great movements, men of a certain caliber.

But nobody I knew was a great white hope, or a hope of any color, really. Nobody I knew aspired to greatness. The people around me generally wanted the riches and relaxation promised to them if they followed the rules, and, mostly, they tried hard to follow them. They put us kids into sports camps, dutifully filling out the scholarship applications to secure our partially funded slots. They told us to listen to our teachers and impress our bosses. Although frequently entangled with the criminal justice system, my family was only vaguely critical of the law. Our rebellions were personal: instead of marching or orating, we drank and drugged ourselves into oblivion, and then, if we could, we clocked into work the next day. We used self-punishing language and policed each other for trashy, off-white behavior, sheathed in a self-protective denial about who we really were. This fantasy was a shining armor we rarely, if ever, took off.

o

The shining denial and armored silence around class meant I never really knew how my family members saw themselves and our context. Did my parents and siblings think we were trash? Recently, during a phone call with my mom, I decided to break the rules.

"Have you ever thought of yourself as white trash?" I asked. I was in my apartment in New York City, where I had moved to attend a prestigious MFA program. She was three thousand miles away in her rental house in Oregon, in a town even smaller and more rural than the ones where I grew up. I was nervous to pose the question because I knew that, like me, she'd probably been hurt by being compared to garbage all her life. I thought that bringing it up would probably sting.

"No," she said, confidently. "In my whole life, I was never that low." At first, it shocked me to hear how firmly she resisted the label while at the same time reifying its derogatory power. Yet, the more I thought about it, the more I understood her need to define herself as above *something*. While I pressed her to explain her reasoning, she mentioned that her dad, who was "a blisters on his hands and blisters on his feet kind of a guy," was always employed, in a relatively coveted job at the mill, and that they lived in a house—not a trailer—that they owned, however modest. I didn't press her about the times she had been unemployed and impoverished as an adult, or about the times some of us had lived in campers and cars, or about the food stamps we qualified for, or about our sleeves of prison tattoos. I didn't want to put my definition of trash into her head. I wanted to hear it from her.

"So what is white trash, then?" I asked.

"I feel like I am being judgey or stereotyping," she said, trying to get out of answering.

"Does it always have to be a bad thing, though?" I looked out my window at the guys selling weed from their cars to escape the cold New England winter. "Couldn't it ever be a good thing, something to reclaim? Like, a point of pride?"

"No, I don't feel like it can."

I didn't let her off the hook. Instead, I asked her to help me understand exactly what the term meant to her so that I could see why it was so bad.

She laughed a little, then directed me to a country song called "Same Trailer, Different Park," which, for her, she said, defines what white trash is. "They live in a trailer park. Mom sells Mary Kay, Dad does Mary Jane *and* Mary the next-door neighbor. The brother doesn't go to school. They're on welfare…" she trailed off. "You know. It's about being in poverty. It's low."

She went on to mention another cultural emblem of our ilk: *8 Mile*, the film in which working-class Rabbit, played by Eminem, struggles to launch a rap career while he toils at a manufacturing plant in Detroit. The film opens with a homeless Rabbit changing out of his barfed-on clothes. He pulls a fresh shirt from a garbage bag he has stored behind a dumpster. We watch him move into his mom's trailer, then struggle to get to work in a series of shitty cars and ill-timed public buses. We watch how, at the end of a long, hard day, he loses his temper at his alcoholic mother or her crappy, abusive boyfriend.

I didn't relate to everything in the movie, and there was plenty with which to take issue, but I certainly recognized the grinding disappointment of impoverishment and the raucous, destructive shenanigans of shooting paintball guns at cop cars and partying in abandoned houses. I particularly loved how the guys in the film torched the house where a little girl had been raped, and which they called an "attractive nuisance," appropriating the law's language and power because they knew the city would not intervene to improve the neighborhood or protect its children. Rabbit and his people were a multiracial squad of trashy people who seemed to have a lot in common with the ways we lived, sometimes fast and hard, sometimes up against the wall, so I still didn't quite understand why Mom resisted it.

Identifying with trash can be fun. Existing in a way that troubles polite society makes for a thrilling fugitivity. Breaking laws, smashing stuff, and bending rules—especially when these acts help you survive—is exhilarating and necessary work. At the same time, being classed as trash can hurt. It can hurt like hunger or like arthritis or like a funeral or a failing grade or a mean joke or a side-eye or like a police baton to the head.

"So were you poor or middle class or what?" I asked. Another lie about trash is that everyone agrees on the parameters of its definition. One man's trash is another man's treasure, and I wondered if my trash was mom's middle class.

"We were somewhere in between," she said. I pressed her on this, having spent quite a bit of time in her rundown childhood house with its DIY concrete driveway, weedy yard, and rusty basketball hoop. When I reminded her of all the times she complained about the crap food she was forced to eat, she backtracked a little.

"I mean we got government cheese."

o

A fridge full of government cheese is one thing that might define trash, but there are plenty of other ways to separate the haves from the have-nots. Later still, my mom defined as trashy the people who lived in the unincorporated country around her town, people who dwelt in squatted sheds, wielded shotguns against trespassers, fucked their siblings, and cooked meth. Through education and travel, I had distanced myself from my white trash upbringing. My concept of trash as a social class had become much more nuanced and even empowering since I left home, but I could see why our perspectives differed so much. She had much more at stake.

I understood how people like my mom might want to distinguish themselves from even poorer, more oppressed groups of trash people. In her forties, Mom earned an associate's degree so that she could work in medical offices in mid-level clerical roles instead of the lowest-paying ones. Now fifty-three years old, she admitted that making more than twenty dollars per hour for the first time in her life made her feel like she was finally somebody.

If I admit I am trash, I get scholarships from institutions and street cred among my artist friends for my tough upbringing. If she admits it, all her hard work, all that striving toward white picket fences and green, green money, means next to nothing. For her, class is still about personal choice, and who would choose to be trash? Absent a political understanding of how race and class function—an understanding that her community college's technical training program was not designed to help her develop—she would be left with no one to blame for her hardship but herself.

My ideas about trash were formed by high-falutin social theory and NPR podcasts, one of which, called *Code Switch*, did a whole episode on the term white trash, which they called "the Swiss army knife of insults" because of the way it not only degrades poor white folks, but also poor people of color, rural people, people without a college degree, and anyone who even acts in stereotypically poor ways. People in these categories fail at being white, or the right kind of white, and they are, therefore, trash.

o

My people were definitely failures at being the right sort of white. Nobody before me held office or started a markedly successful business. Nobody in my family ever published a book or, as far as I know, even an article in the newspaper. Nobody was a deacon or a teacher or a pillar of the community. We worked our jobs and tried to take care of ourselves and each other and that's it until we died. The good life imagined by my family was not one of revolution, justice, or artistic expression. The most valuable skill was earning enough money to stay alive.

We were losers. We lost body parts in workplace accidents. We lost our minds and ended up in mental hospitals. We lost years of our lives behind bars. We lost jobs and then we lost the cars we couldn't pay for. We lost weight from lack of nutrition or a preponderance of speed. We lost our color, our white necks reddened by the sun, our faces and hands smeared with the singe of grease and dirt.

Every weeknight plus Saturdays while I was in middle and high school, my dad worked his shift at the auto parts store. By the time I was twelve, he had worked his way up to a middle-management role with a livable salary, but that didn't spare him long days traversing concrete floors, helping customers at the counter and in the parking lot in front of the store. When he got home each night, he parked the sensible, used Toyota sedan—the baby blue one with a crushed front fender that never got fixed because he used the insurance money to take us to Disneyland—then came in through the laundry room. He changed out of his work uniform and slipped on a coat.

He would grab a Budweiser from the refrigerator and say, "How do you like me now?" while he stuck his tongue out and opened his eyes wide. He would shake his can in the air, miming drunk. Then he would walk out to the garage where he drank his beers or, on more difficult days, plastic cups full of bottom-shelf liquor cut with a dash of mixer, and smoke Marlboro red cigarettes while he tinkered with something mechanical, watered the half-bald lawn, or watched my brother ride his BMX bike up and down the street as the lights blinked yellow in the growing darkness. The subdivision where we lived then abutted the city limit. Untamed country and gravel roads loomed in the night beyond the lamps.

Sometimes he would be out there long past sunset. From my bedroom, where I hunched over my homework or studied the inserts from my favorite CDs, I'd hear the door open and then close behind him as he came back into the house.

"Tired, old man?" I'd yell, my version of goodnight.

"I'll sleep when I'm dead."

o

My dad always said, "I'll sleep when I'm dead," but I was still too young to relate to this particular type of exhaustion. I was, however, growing tired of trying to fit myself in with the straight-laced, middle-class kids. On the first day of my freshman year, I dressed myself in what I had guessed would be the "it" shoe of the season. I wore white Pumas with clear soles, a pair of wide-leg denim overalls, and a white zip-up hoodie with hibiscus flowers up the arms and a gigantic Roxy logo on its chest. The shoes were the one thing we could afford that could make people think I wasn't white trash. I tried my best with the clothes, which I shopped for on sale racks, in friend's closets, and, on special occasions, at the malls in bigger towns.

A few weeks before that September morning, Dad drove me and my best friend Lynnsy to an outlet mall on the Oregon coast to do our school clothes shopping. Lynnsy had been one of the popular girls I both feared and idolized in early middle school. I watched the cute boys who played soccer and lived on the good side of town follow her through the halls like hot baby ganders behind a goose, their frosted tips gelled up toward the sky like tail feathers. Lynnsy had something about her that made people want her, and I had studied her in ten-second bursts, trying to discern what she did to be so alluring. Later, I would learn that this something likely came from growing up with a mother who did sex work.

Lynnsy's mom was a woman who knew how to use tricks of light and sleights of hand to protect herself, as much as possible, from being trashed and criminalized. Instead of using her body to perform manual labor, she dressed it up in glittering outfits and twirled on a stage, high above the men who came to worship at her feet. She was beguiling, a queen of the strip club rack, a self-employed, self-possessed woman who, with the good grace of her fellow performers, had dug herself out of a trash heap town not unlike the one Lynnsy by the straps of her shiny high heels.. She had traded up from one kind of trashy to a better, glitzier version. Lynnsy became heir to this legacy, part of which was a survivalist charm that meant she could get what she needed, could have a good life despite being bad according to polite company's rules, and despite being relatively uneducated, racially ambiguous, and a little bit crazy.

We became friends in seventh grade after Lynnsy invited me over to her house one day on a dare. While I helped her do her after-school chores, we talked about our lives and found we had a lot in common. We both lived with our single fathers, a rare arrangement in any town, and a fact that made us feel special in a bad way, like freaks. Our moms, who were both young and with whom we had once had good relationships, struggled with addiction, so were absent from our lives for great swaths of time, including the first three years of our friendship. Our dads worked almost constantly—hers as a stud welder—and so, a year and a half later, we were already inseparable. And we were going to go shopping.

The plain storefronts at the outlet mall, with their tinted windows and *30% OFF SALE!* posters, surrounded the parking lot, bearing back-lit signs that read Nautica, Famous Footwear, Big Dogs, Old Navy, and Billabong in bold, square lettering—hardly the hottest stores, but something to work with. We bought capri pants, tight t-shirts, fresh white sneakers, and quarter-zip sweaters. While standing in line with the clothing I had picked out for the year, I prayed that I had made the right choices, that I might blend in so much as to become invisible. When my dad put his bank card on the counter, I felt guilty for needing anything. How many days did he have to work to make the hundred dollars he had spent on me in seconds? I didn't know how the numbers worked, but I knew my clothes cost a lot.

On the first day of school, my mom made a special trip to my dad's house, where I was living then, so that she could drop me off. She had wanted me to feel special, maybe a little bit like a princess, and princesses didn't take the bus. She arrived in a beat-up car I'd never seen, and I tried to hide my disappointment at its raggedy appearance. We drove the back way, along the railroad tracks, then through an older neighborhood that led into a couple blocks of apartments and fast food restaurants. As we idled at a red light at the intersection of 58th and Main streets, a block from school, the car stuttered, wheezed, and died, despite mom working the gas pedal. I smelled fumes. I didn't want to look my mom in the face, so I looked at the older teens smoking cigarettes next to the 7-11, a spot we would later dub the Smoking Tree—kingdom of the kids who lived in trailer parks and huffed household aerosols through rags.

"It's ok," my mom said, forcing a smile that I could hear over the cars accelerating around us. I still couldn't turn to look at her. She pointed to the gas station in the strip mall to our left. "I can push it right over there. No problem." It was true that I had seen her—I had even helped her—push our shitty cars down busy streets before. I said a little prayer to myself, *please, god, don't make me do this,* but I knew it would be my duty, as a good daughter, to help her if she asked. She didn't ask. Instead, she urged me to hurry up and git goin', lest I be late. With embarrassingly little coaxing, I left her there in that broken-down car and walked myself to school, humiliated and angry, sure that everyone saw right through the facade I had tried to construct out of white leather and outlet mall cotton. As I walked the long, gray block to school, into the next chapter of my life, a chapter that was already turning out to be just as punishing and difficult as the one before, I braced myself against what might come later from classmates who, I was sure, would use my morning's misfortune to talk trash.

Nobody seemed to notice or care about the car, but the incident broke something in me. As the year progressed, I dropped the preppy act and the desperation for acceptance by the popular kids. On weekends, Lynnsy and I stopped pulling our brown hair through the beauty supply store bleach cap, which, in concert with the white-blue chemical powder, we had used to streak our hair white. Instead, we dyed our hair in darker colors, maroons and browns that mimicked the colors of the oil spots in our driveways. Over the course of our ninth-grade year, I started skateboarding, and I stopped going to church, and I replaced the Jewel CD in my Discman with Green Day's *Dookie*.

By the end of the year, we had even embraced thrift shopping. At Value Village, we combed the racks for clothes that would irritate and confound the people around us. We found a teeny X-Men shirt that perverted boyhood fun with the way it highlighted our burgeoning tits, and a neon red tube skirt we could pull up well past a good, modest length. We found hoodies that we cut up, sewed tighter, and drew on, customizing our looks. Long, baggy shorts sagged at my waist, still soft with baby fat.

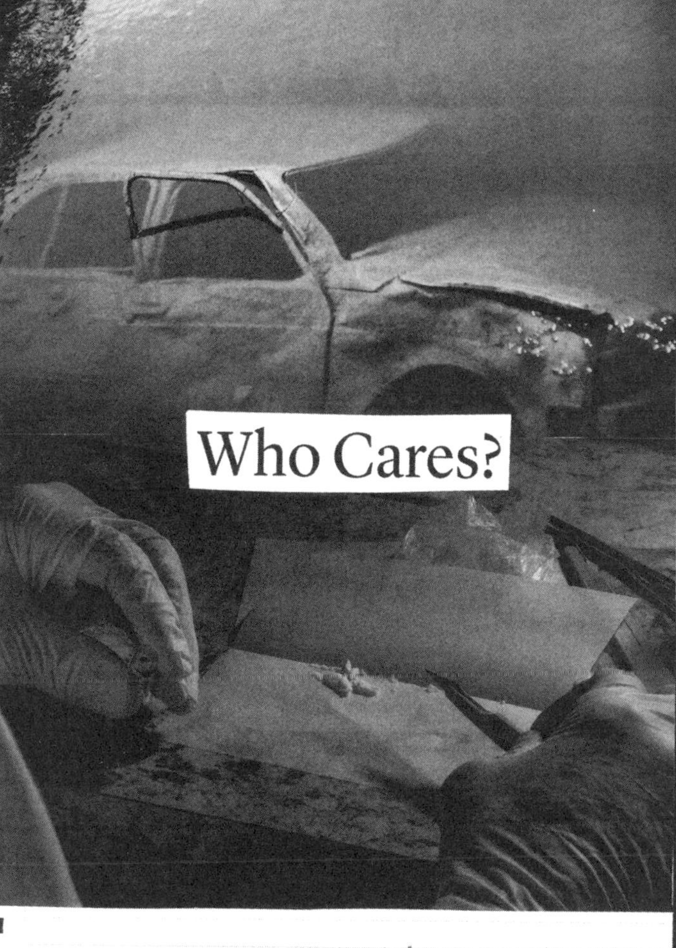
Who Cares?

We bought anything that looked like it came from a Hot Topic or the lost and found at a dive bar. What I once found humiliating—wearing old, off-brand, off-trend clothing—was becoming a badge of courage, and a fuck you to polite society. I was done feeling bad about my lack of money, status, and good name. It was thrilling to wear weird, inappropriate clothing. My trashy rags became a freak flag I flew with a swell of pride in my chest.

Every morning that year, I got up for school and put on ever-more provocative outfits. I packed my lunch, if I planned on eating at all, then woke my little brother on my way out the door. Dad had already left for the day, and it was still dark when, at 6:45, I walked up the hill and stood at the city limit on the country highway to wait for my school bus. Across the road, our neighbors had built a beautiful wraparound porch for their double-wide trailer, which they painted by hand and appointed with pots of petunias and plastic lawn furniture. Another, smaller trailer with rust spots stood on the other side of their gravel driveway, and a yellow *BEWARE of DOG* sign glowed in the dim morning light on the low, chain link fence. Now I can see the mundane glory in growing such a life from hard work and good luck, but then, the aluminum trailers and unruly yards stood for difficulty, lack, and a failure to thrive.

All was quiet on the road, except for the occasional rooster or passing car, but I had my headphones on and the music turned up full blast. Green Day's storm of drums and vocals numbed me to the day ahead and drew squiggly lines around the anguish I felt. I began to own my cynicism and ugliness, rather than trying to hide it. As I kicked rocks across the asphalt, I sang along:

"Pay attention to the cracked streets
And the broken homes
Some call it slums
Some call it nice
I want to take you through
A wasteland I like to call my home
Welcome to paradise"

o

Because home was a wasteland, I thought I'd find paradise through books. Education, I was told, would be my golden ticket out. I got good grades, sat still in class, and showed some academic promise, so I was placed in every one of the few advanced courses offered by my school.

With the desperation of the dying, I devoted myself to my studies. In my 10th grade AP US History class, I sat at a table etched with little drawings of dicks and the initials of lover + lover carved inside cartoon hearts. An infinite trickle of rain leaked through holes in the ceiling of our classroom, down among the pipes and wires, and then found the seams between the white ceiling tiles and their flimsy metal frames where it snuck out and then fell, sometimes on our heads. Next to me, a trash can slowly filled with grimy water. There were three or four cans positioned strategically around Mr. Smith's small classroom. The drips provided a syncopated background music for his more monotone lectures. *Piece of garbage school,* I thought, as I bent to read from my decades-old textbook, its margins scummy with years of gray graphite scribbles. My maternal grandma had attended this same school, and I once flipped to the front cover of my book to study the annual student checkout record, half expecting to find her name there. All that fall and winter and into the spring, I sat and studied with the drip, drip, dripping.

Nobody in my extended family had ever left this small town, and because I found it so depressing and loathsome, I could not figure out why, though I held suspicions. One was that nobody seemed to have, or see, or even want any other choice. After graduating from my high school forty years before me, my grandma had worked intermittently as a housekeeper and raised three children. I never asked my grandma, but I assume nobody ever told her she had promise, and even if they had, who knows if that would've been enough to make any difference.

Similarly, my mom wanted to be a dental hygienist or, better yet, to have a husband with enough income that she could be a stay-at-home mom. There's nothing wrong with being a mom or a maid, but I sensed that the decisions my family was making were not choices so much as compromises or fates to which one should resign. The grown folks in my life seemed to have low self-esteem and low expectations. To become anything besides a low-down, good-for-nothin' criminal or a marginally employed welfare case was to win at a game with improbable odds, like coming away victorious from a marksmanship challenge at a state fair, lugging a neon pink bear the size of a twelve-year-old child. I had to believe that school would save me, would bring prizes beyond what I could even envision.

Even though Mr. Smith's teaching style was more sleepy than sexy, Lynnsy and I liked him. We often stayed after class for a few minutes to talk with him. Lynnsy flirted and secured extensions or higher grades on various homework assignments. I asked him questions about riots and uprisings, anarchists and martyrs, anything from class that caught my interest. Lynnsy and I were both eager to please in our own ways. Mr. Smith acted kindly and never broke his professional posture. His favorite thing to talk to us about was punk—his twenty-something son was in a band. He asked us permutations of this question over and over:

"Have you guys ever been to a Rancid concert?"
"You guys get any new Rancid CDs?"
"How 'bout that 'Roots Radicals,' huh?"

It seemed like Rancid was the only band he knew. Even though we were starting to outgrow and even scorn poppier artists like them, we humored Mr. Smith. We *had* been to a Rancid concert, and we told him how we'd waited in line all day so that we could be up front, close enough to the stage to get spit on by the lead singer, and how the surge of the crowd had pressed us against the metal barricades so forcefully that we almost blacked out.

Punk appealed to me because of its ugliness, its rage, and its rejection of Christian dogma, mall culture, mainstream politics, and everything else that hated us. I was hungry to hate right back. In the absence of a silver spoon or divine intervention, I was going to be a loser. Punk gave me a way to claim my trashiness and turn up the volume to eleven. Finally, after years of not fitting in, I was starting to unfit myself. I felt in control of how trashy I was.

Before I could fully own my trashiness, I first had to define it. I needed to know what I could claim and what I should reject. Besides what I gleaned from church, schools, and television, I had been learning how to do this through clothes. The Swedish word *trasa* refers to rags or tatters and is counted as an etymological relative of our trash. My *trasa* were the ripped-up, patched-up, too-short, too-tight, or too-big thrift store clothes and band t-shirts that I had begun to wear with such offensive assertiveness.

I colored my hair black and then scorched it white-yellow. I dyed it teal, then purple, then cherry red, and shaved the sides so that only a mohawk remained. I wore scissor-slashed fishnets, sweatshirts covered in patches, and eye makeup so thick and black that my eyes became bright-centered holes. I tattooed messy stick-and-pokes into my skin with sewing needles and calligraphy ink. I cut the shortest, sluttiest skirts imaginable from old tank tops, and styled them in the ugliest way I could, flaunting my bruises and bones. I dared men to objectify me, to see through the mess and filth to the sex blooming beneath my angst. In this ragged, screaming way, I was inspired by the people in the punk bands to which I had become so devoted, especially the women who had fought for my right to be ugly and angry, tattered and critical.

o

I was ugly and angry and inspired by the punks, but I was also inspired by some of the people in my 10th-grade history book, especially those who had fought for my right to sit in a classroom, even one that leaked and lacked so much. I knew that if I had been born just a few generations earlier, I would not have made it to high school. At fifteen, I would have been working full time in the fields or as a cook or housekeeper, possibly carrying my first child, which is exactly what my great-grandmother who sent her daughter to this high school had done not even sixty years prior. I was not the first person in my family to graduate from high school, but I would be the first who would be able to pursue higher education. Both Mom and Dad admitted they weren't the book learnin' kind when, by high school, my homework became too difficult for them to help me, which they rarely had the time or energy to do anyway. While I labored over trigonometry problems and end-of-chapter essay questions, they made self-deprecating jokes and admonished me to be nothing like them. Or if not nothing, better. Hence, the AP course.

In Mr. Smith's class, I read about people like Emma Goldman, the anarcho-feminist. In the mug-shot for her arrest for "Inciting a Riot," taken when she was wrongly implicated in the assassination of President McKinley, Emma Goldman looks raggedy.

Her bun is loose and wind-blown and her glasses are held on by a thick string that crisscrosses wildly over her neck and chest.

Goldman started an anarchist journal called *Mother Earth* in 1906 and was its first editor. Like her live-action activism, which often got her dragged off to jail or slandered in the newspapers, the journal concerned itself with all manner of liberatory, even proto-punk content: labor rights, education-for-all, draft-dodging, women's emancipation, birth control, and most of all, sexual freedom, which was central to her idea of revolution. I was obsessed with her.

I didn't explore queerness much then, except through the conventionally ugly, genderfuck outfits I wore and the cute girl that I made out with on prom night. But me and my friends trashed rules about gender and sexuality on the regular. Shea, whip-smart, red-headed, and trailer-raised, had girlfriends *and* boyfriends. Luke, who wore costumes and had two moms, and Nick, one of the few obviously-gay guys at our school, both used eye makeup, dyed their hair, and fucked each other in the bathroom. I had failed out of the upper echelons of the small-town social register and into this chosen family. We loved each other, sometimes erotically, and always in a way that made our bad town feel like paradise. My friends and I all failed at being good girls and good boys, so we became something else instead.

The author Vivian Gornick said of Goldman, "Hers was the sensibility not of the intellectual but of the artist; and she performed like an artist, dramatizing for others what they could hardly articulate for themselves." She inspired in people a "wild, vagrant hope." Goldman found art and sex integral to the revolution, which is why her joyless life as an exhausted immigrant sweatshop worker moved her to rebellion. Demeaning labor, she said, estranged people from their feelings and made "free love" impossible. Her idea of this love was capacious, queer, and total. At fifteen, I had never heard anything like it except, maybe, on a punk record.

I could not dream of being a writer then or of making any mark on the world aside from the occasional anarchy symbol scrawled onto my aging desk. It never crossed my mind that I might be published in a journal or magazine, which I can now say that I have, let alone start or edit one as Goldman did. I didn't know I would try to write something different about women and whores and trash. I needed to be taught, slowly, over time, mostly by my fellow rejects, how to envision an alternate future, just as I was taught to be ready for a long life of toil and disappointment, punctuated by the occasional joy: a raise, a vacation to California, a few grandkids, even a pastor's promise of the spoils that awaited me (if I was good enough) in heaven. I no longer believed in god or middle-class comfort, but I needed to believe that a college education could save me from the worst of the pain I saw around me, even though it was not clear how it might. Education, I was sure, could be a kind of freedom. I wasn't sure what the future held, but by studying history and literature and art, at least I could have an understanding of the past, leveraging what I learned to make something radical of my life. I wanted to know everything, however hurtful the truth often was.

o

The truth in any tense is often hurtful, and so is the truth about the origins of our language. Both the noun and the verb "trash" are recorded to have "obscure" beginnings in the *Oxford English Dictionary*, perhaps because nobody bothered to write down—or rather publish—this particular history. Trash is a noun, but it is also a verb whose origins are obliterative. Along with the Swedish *trasa*, another probable ancestor of trash is the French verb *trasier* meaning "to draw a line through, strike out, efface." I imagine all the lives that had already been effaced before trash entered the English lexicon in 1604—forever crowning and denigrating Bianca, the slut, the accused criminal, the patron saint of a certain class of erotic love.

The *OED*'s entry also mentions "field trash," the dried leaves that remain around the base of sugarcanes after harvest. This kind of trash is also brutal: it has bloodied the hands of last century's enslaved Africans and this century's exploited farmworkers. In the dictionary's discussion, the word *trash* can refer to worn-out shoes donned by tramps and vagrants. Elsewhere in the word's origin, chips fly from axes wielded in the rough hands of backwoods loggers, since *trash* also means that which is cast off from tree-felling. As one works through the etymology, one encounters all sorts of laborers trashed by exhausting work, filthy and ragged, thrashing through mire and dirt.

I learned these definitions in books and in dictionaries, like the one in which I found that one obsolete usage of the verb *to trash* means to hold back, restrain, or hinder. Everything that has trashed me over the years—not just my years, but the years that led up to me—the demeaning work, the name-calling, the looming threats of hunger and incarceration—held me back from something I can't yet name, but that I am inching toward, slowly, the more I learn.

o

The more I learn, the freer I become, but I also get angrier, uglier, and more critical. While completing my third college degree, fifteen years after my sophomore year of high school, I took a class from the great-grand-something of Harriet Beecher Stowe, the famed abolitionist. My teacher, a carefully dressed, classically professorial sort of woman, took great pride in her literary lineage. She told us about her family's legacy in the arts when she introduced herself on the first day.

Beecher Stowe, like my teacher, wrote many acclaimed books and essays in her lifetime. In them, she made impassioned arguments against slavery using vivid narrative techniques and thorough research. She also did it by railing against white trash people—scourge of the American South.

Beecher Stowe dedicated an entire chapter to my people, the garbage gang, when she wrote her second book, *The Key to Uncle Tom's Cabin* in 1854. The chapter is entitled, simply, "Poor White Trash." She writes, "These miserable families grow up heathen on a Christian soil, in idleness, vice, dirt, and discomfort of all sorts. They are the pest of the neighborhood, the scoff and contempt or pity even of the slaves." This describes my ancestors, and, frankly, me and my contemporaries, we a whole trashy kingdom of despicable peasants.

Harriet Beecher Stowe blamed slavery for the creation of our mongrel class because of the way it concentrated wealth with plantation-owning elites, leaving poorer whites to languish on infertile, backwoods plots with no way to earn a proper living or get an education. Other intellectuals in her time believed that poor white trash were their own race entirely, the result of bad blood poisoned by generations of immorality, inbreeding, or interracial relationships. Similarly, she described white trash as more "degraded and miserable" than even the enslaved people with whom they were ridiculed for associating.

My college teacher was deeply intelligent, quite accomplished, and mostly very kind. She taught her favorite works from the Western canon in an organized, passionate way. Her course was framed as one in which we students could read and discuss the greatest writers who ever lived. We were to read with an eye toward craft so that we might attempt to replicate some of what these great masters of the written word composed.

Like most works in the canon, all the books she chose for us were by or about wealthy people or those aspiring to be so. Their content was generally dismissive or abusive regarding women, the poor, and people of color. While reading *Madame Bovary*, I planted a yellow flag on each page that made direct reference to these groups in unflattering ways. In the end, my copy of the book was radiant with yellow strips, each one a warning against too much self-identification.

Another of the books we read was *House of Mirth*, which was about a woman who would rather die than be poor, who in fact did die because of it. Lily Bart was obsessed with dinginess, with avoiding the horrible, gray life of working-class girls. Like many of her modern-day counterparts, working a thankless job and living in a boarding house turned Lily Bart into a drug addict, then into a drug casualty. Emma Bovary also died from the fear of being poor; the possibility scared her to death.

I do not begrudge my teacher for choosing these texts, nor for having us read them in such an apolitical, white way. I believe she intended to help us be better artists. I am only saying that I was bored and a little hurt by yet another repetition of these same tired tropes.

White, good.

Money, good.

Servants and sluts, bad.

The repetition of these cultural truths even felt oddly affirming. Although they had a cruel way of showing it, the authors of these books knew how hard it was to be poor, especially poor and woman, and they put that truth in black ink on white paper. They saw me, and they described a near-version of my reality. Like *Mirth*'s Bart, I had worked menial jobs, lived in crowded, dark rooms, and spent money I didn't have at fancy restaurants. I had taken too much alcohol and other analgesics to dull the soreness of my existence. I had dulled myself nearly to death. These authors knew that poor and dead have a close kinship.

o

Poor and dead had also been kin in AP US History, where I finished reading a section about the Haymarket Massacre and the struggle for the eight-hour workday, then paused to stare at my reflection in the trash can of water next to my desk. I was careful not to get any of the liquid on my arms or head—Mr. Smith had warned us about the possibility of asbestos. As I stared at a slice of my face in the rippling water, I considered that many of our parents could not find jobs that offered full-time hours or paid a living wage. What use is an eight-hour workday when there is no workday to work, or when the wage on offer is a violation of one's humanity? Living in a trash town, the prevailing feeling is nihilism.

In my headphones between classes, the Sex Pistols screamed, "When there's no future, how can there be sin? We're the flowers in the dustbin." On the school bus home while meth labs and vacant lots slid in and out of view, Crass made a ruckus like banging hard and fast on trash can lids, singing "Do they owe us a living? 'Course they fucking do!" On weekends, I went to punk shows and jumped into the mosh pit. All my losses, failures, and fears dissolved when I took the first elbow to the face. What went on outside the show ceased to matter, and I fell out of reality, into what the more monied parents might have called *the wrong crowd*.

We chugged wine from bags and Mad Dog 20/20 bottles. We smoked all kinds of stuff. We sucked dicks in the back seats of cars. We refused to bathe. We worked the jobs that would have us: fast food, mostly. Ugly, stinky jobs for ugly, stinky people who just wanted to earn enough to be able to buy gas, go to shows, and black out.

That same year, the school, in a budget crisis, asked us to bring in toilet and printer paper. We had run out. *Piece of trash school,* I thought, as I stuffed a couple of bargain toilet tissue rolls into my backpack to drop off at the front office. The bathroom stalls mostly had toilet paper that year, and we made do when the copies dried up. The roof never fell in, and I wasn't fatally poisoned by asbestos. I moved away, and I went to college, but I could not shake the image of the trash can and me in my classroom.

o

Later, I learned I could draw a line from my trash can and me in my classroom all the way back to 14th-century England. White trash was not a new idea when Beecher Stowe popularized it. Poor and trash, like poor and dead, had been related for centuries, in Shakespeare's time and before, ever since colonial England needed exploitable labor to power its empire, and a linguistic ideology to buttress its mission. British colonizers filled ships with thousands of the kingdom's poor people—mostly Scots, Irish, and Welsh—to work as indentured servants in the so-called New World. These "waste people" were seen as unproductive vagrants, perfect for dumping into a short, brutal life of hard labor developing the land as it was cleared, by genocide, of indigenous Americans. For a long time after, there were at least as many white trash as enslaved Africans in what is now the United States. The landed class used trash to divide the working class, and to create a separate, dingier world for whites who did not meet their standards of racial supremacy. The term made dehumanization easy and was, ultimately, effective.

The opposite of trash in Shakespeare's 1604 was the nobility. The king and queen and the rest of the small class of royals held the money, waged the wars, and generally ran the show. The waste people at the bottom were the worst of the worst of the poor, who found themselves without food and shelter. Because their numbers had increased in the century prior, due in part to all the wealth the nobility hoarded, the royal family passed new Poor Laws to "assist" them, updating statues first codified in 1349. Workhouses and other institutions sprang up to corral, control, and extract labor from these "vagrants" and "helpless cases." Under one iteration of these codes, a poor person who refused a day's work could be executed by the state. Or, I suppose, they were indentured in the colonies.

My father's elders were Okies on one side and Blacksmiths from Norway on the other. My mother's lineage is more mongrel and mysterious—her origin story includes infidelity, adoptions, and run-aways—but my maternal great-grandma, who was Scots-Irish and Welsh, lived until I was in my twenties, and I suspect she hailed from England's trash can classes.

Beecher Stowe would've called Granny white trash. Her kith and kin were musicians, drunks, and petty criminals. Not book-crackers, skull-crackers. Progeny of waste people, ignobles. She had babies with four different men, survived domestic violence, drank, smoked, and yelled. She cooked with Crisco and shopped for clothes at St. Vincent de Paul. But she was also a white trash class traitor, according to Stowe's definition, in that she refused to condemn other poor people, including Black people and migrant farm workers. Granny regularly cussed at the TV over anti-welfare rhetoric, slights against unions, or racist dog whistles—probably a rare quality in a white woman born in the 1920s. I believe that Granny believed that the working class were the true nobility. I believe she had confidence, that she was a glitch in the system, a queer element.

Granny's real name was Hester Ann, but early in her life, she changed it to Anna Mae, for reasons I am unable to discover. My mom guesses Granny found the name Hester unattractive. I tell her that Hester Prynne was the chick from *Scarlet Letter*—a slut in the woods who was forced to wear the big fat A that marked her a dirty woman. Granny had only an eighth-grade education, so it is unlikely that she ever read Hawthorne. It still pleases me to think of her as part of a legacy of women who disturbed the order, who dragged the good name of women in the muck of sensuality, who trashed the rules, however imperfectly.

Today, when people say *white trash*, they are talking about white people who shop at Walmart, fix their own cars, and frequent drive-thru's. They mean whites who live next door to Black and brown people, who work with them as security guards, janitors, clerks, and prep cooks. They mean jailhouse whites. They mean whites who do not speak the Queen's English or Shakespeare's English or anything close to it. They mean white people who are bad at being white. White trash people are still generally understood to be lazy, fat, racist, abusive, alcoholic, dull, tacky, violent, backward, loud, Bible-thumping, and uneducated. Such stereotypes are kept alive by television, political policy, miseducation, and art.

o

Stereotypes about sex workers are also kept alive by a culture whose ideology hasn't evolved all that much in the five hundred years since *Othello* first played out on the stage. Lynnsy would grow up to be a sex worker, as did one of my sisters, an aunt, a cousin, and perhaps many others who chose to remain anonymous, even to friends or relatives. My loved ones have danced for many years at clubs where they made good money performing, but their athleticism and beauty were not recognized outside the dark halls of the strip clubs and drag shows. Besides dancing, I don't know what other work they have done, and I won't ask. Even if I did ask, I wouldn't write it down. These people are precious to me, but my opinions about their worth aren't enough to protect them from further violence. They have already been ridiculed, beaten, threatened, stalked, and, like ur-trash Bianca, jailed for reclaiming their bodies from the state and daring to make a living as sole proprietors of their own queer business.

The artist Tatiana Luboviski-Acosta defines trash as "the precariat" a "portmanteau of 'precarious' and 'proletariat.'" Not "the mythical white working class," but those who are marked as even more worthless than white and working: sex workers, the incarcerated, the formally unemployed, the undocumented, the disabled, the not-white. "In short," Luboviski-Acosta writes, "trash is a political position of abject disenfranchisement… To be trash is to not be pandered to, or courted. To be trash is to be forgotten, disposed of, razed, evicted, poisoned, gaslit. Policed. It is to be detained, incarcerated, deported, murdered." To this list, one might add scapegoated, blamed, and made to lose.

o

I didn't want to be forgotten, razed, evicted, poisoned, gaslit, scapegoated, blamed, or made to lose, so I had mimed being a winner: a middle-class white girl who would assume a respectable position in society, perhaps as an educator. When I was little, I often played teacher with my stuffed animals. I loved reading aloud to my eager legion of pastel pupils, some hand-me-down, some store-bought, who sat silently in a circle on my bed. I gave them spelling tests and writing assignments. I read to them from my favorite books such as *The Boxcar Children* and *Where the Red Fern Grows.* Like most of the books I liked then, these titles featured protagonists who were lowlives in some way—bums, orphans, rednecks, charity cases—characters with whom I could connect. In my private life, I fancied myself a precocious, bold adventurer, a resourceful backwoods hero, a rebellious flower child.

But the books I loved were also rife with clumsy tropes and thinly veiled classism that molded my little brain into a self-loathing machine. In *Where the Red Fern Grows,* the protagonist's father is "a good, honest farmer. He is poor, but he is working hard so his family can move to the city." His mother is "part-Cherokee" and, like Pa, "wants very much to move to town so the children can get a good education." From this story, I understood that poor people, Indigenous Americans, and country folk should aspire to be their opposite. Similarly, the *Boxcar Children* are orphans on the run from a grandpa they believe to be cruel, but the series ends happily when the siblings reunite with him, and he turns out to be a rich, magnanimous gentleman. In each of these books, the poor kids' lives are inadequate, but they are promised salvation by wealthy, high-brow outsiders. I didn't think I could ever be rich, but I could move to the city and get a "good education." I could even be the one giving it.

I had my doubts about becoming a teacher because, in some ways, I was still licking my school-wrought wounds when, at twenty-six years old, I decided to apply to get a graduate degree in K-12 education. School had been the site of a lot of pain for me, good as I was, and it hadn't helped me materially as much as people promised. Moreover, I still had my facial piercings, dyed hair, tattoos, and bad attitude. I still smoked cigarettes—an unquestionably déclassée behavior by 2015, particularly for women who spent any part of their day with children. I was into self-publishing and auto-didacts, oral histories, and outsider artists. I had studied unschooling and other alternative educational philosophies. I had spent considerable energy in college avoiding classes that lionized the canon and its wealthy, white power. I hesitated to become a teacher because no matter how much I have loved school, it has never truly loved me back.

o

School didn't love me back, but I was used to being in places where I didn't belong. Despite what I knew about the difficulties of teaching in the public school system, I wanted to try. I hoped to carve out a liberated, caring space for students who felt like they didn't fit, and to organize for causes such as the abolition of the school-to-prison pipeline, then the hottest issue in education. My brother and older sister both earned GEDs after drop-outs and expulsions, in addition to encounters with the legal system. At least, I thought, I could see the beauty and potential in kids trashed by the schools, the courts, and the violence of low-income, off-white life. I thought maybe if I was the good kind of bad—the agitator kind—then maybe I could enjoy it. At the very least, I could fuck shit up.

It shocked me how quickly I lost my vision. Ultimately, I found that I was the one getting glitched or, on the worst days, *trasier*'ed. Teaching was trashing work and I was not strong enough to resist the ideological discipline endemic to the technology of the public school with its ability tracking and required courses, with its referrals and suspensions. By the end of my short career as a full-time teacher in public schools, I was as exhausted as my parents ever were, despite my entrée into white-collar work.

I taught my first three years in a high school that was much nicer than the one I had attended. It was tucked away in the hills on the west side of town, amid winding lanes of beautiful, historic homes. The wealthier segment of the parent community, composed of neurosurgeons, psychiatrists, professors, and heirs to successful family businesses, was very giving. The school's annual auction raised tens of thousands of dollars for special programs and school improvements. Not all the students at the school were well-off, but the school never ran out of paper as mine had, nor did its roof leak into strategically placed garbage cans. I was intimidated by these parents, who were rumored to be litigious and obsessed with academic rigor.

Early in my first year of teaching, I made space for my students to do creative work. First, we made zines about our lives, and then I had them make playlists, from which they analyzed songs of their choosing, rather than write essays about some dusty old novel or play. When I chose class readings, I took care to include works by members of the "precariat" classes, so that my kids could form a more generous conception of these groups than I had been encouraged to—whether they identified with them or not. But I didn't stay good for long. The daily challenges of teaching high school bled me of my convictions. My boss, a mean, white-blonde assistant principal, told me to get control of my classes, and a district-provided mentor agreed. I spent late afternoons calling parents and long evenings planning lessons I hoped would be engaging, but nothing seemed to work out for anyone involved.

Slowly at first, then quickly, I became a dictator. I sent students to the principal's office for refusing to sit in their assigned seats. I enforced asinine rules regarding the proper use of the hall pass. The very students with whom I had hoped to relate were the victims of my ineptitude, and many stopped coming to my class. As my energy and confidence flagged, I even threw out fun or radical project ideas in favor of the boring, canned curriculum provided by the district, the kind of curriculum to which I had been subjected.

To that end, I taught Shakespeare in Senior English my first year, as recommended by some list of required 12th-grade texts, from which I chose *Othello*, a play I had read for the first time during my graduate program only a year prior. This was around the 2016 election, and I tried to have students read the play with an eye toward rhetoric that betrayed the characters' racist, sexist, and classist attitudes. My smart, capable students hated the way the characters in the play treated women, especially the courtesans, and the only Black character. My smart, capable students also thought the play was boring, old, and a waste of their time. I wonder if they felt our reading lacked appropriate criticality, despite my bumbling attempts. I wonder if any of them felt wronged personally by my insistence that we read something from the canon, which I did for several reasons, one of which was to pass as someone who had never cleaned the fryer at a Taco Bell or scrubbed a stranger's toilet, but who instead had spent all of her time studying Shakespeare in her classes at an elite university.

o

I am not saying that my literature teacher wronged me personally when she insisted we study works that demeaned poor women and workers who got dirty. I am saying she made no living amends for her great-grand-something's legacy, that in subtle ways, she kept her classism alive. I am saying we learn how to think about ourselves by looking at our reflections, especially in books. Especially in garbage cans filled with murky water.

Today, if I could, I would go back to that classroom at the end of the hallway in the shitty school in my shitty hometown and I would rewrite everything in upside-down letters to imbue it with opposite meaning. I would pick up the trash can and stare into the water. From the reflection in the ripples, I would divine a soft future for all the trash kids of this scraggly kingdom of gravel roads, sagging duplexes, and tall grasses. I'd dump the water out the window, then set the empty garbage can on my head, tilted back so I could feel the sun on my face. "Look," I would say. "Inverted, it's almost a crown."

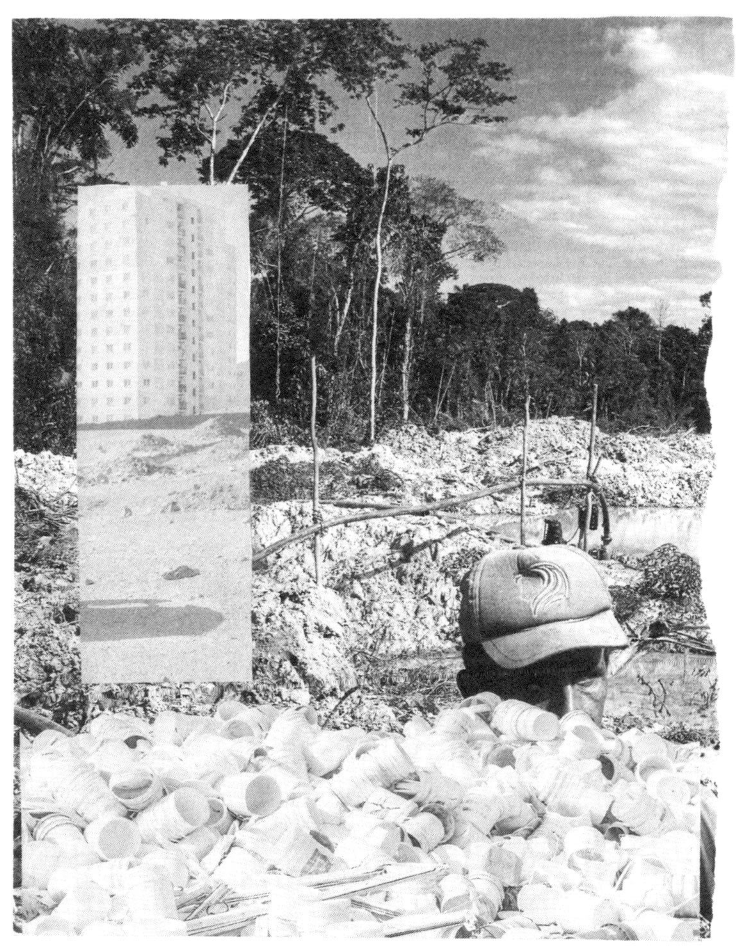

RITUALS TO SEE TRASH #2

1. Go to Walmart. Walk slowly down each aisle, considering the materials required to make the available products. Try to imagine the individuals who assembled them in the factories. Every 60 seconds, pause in front of a shelf. Take a picture of one item that calls to you. Repeat until you've traversed the whole store.

2. Before you leave, go to the photo department and have the images printed. Take the photos to a landfill or dump. Carry a large sack. When you see an item that matches a photo, pick it up and put it in your sack. Repeat until your sack is full.

3. Back at home, display your Walmart photos around the area where you keep your garbage can. Affix them to the outsides of the bin, inside the cupboards, and on the walls. Watch the photos degrade at the pace at which landfilled waste decomposes.

4. It is up to you what to do with the objects. You might arrange them inside a cabinet or create an altar. You might hold a funeral service and bury them in your yard. You might place them back on the shelves in Walmart, noting how long it takes for security to remove you from the premises.

OTHER PEOPLE'S TOILETS

Clad in teal-green work pants and a matching shirt, the artist Mierle Laderman Ukeles stands on an open waste cell at the Fresh Kills Landfill, listening to a man with a large, low belly talk about his work. He wears the same outfit as she does, though his is band-aid beige. He talks with his hands, emphatically, as if he rarely gets an audience. Behind them, three trucks traverse a vast expanse of compacted, brown garbage that reaches the smoggy horizon, above which loom the shrouded outlines of brick buildings. Next to them, a fresh pile of construction debris and disused furniture collapses in on itself. Much of the garbage at the dump is already digested into the filthy olio underfoot, but in this pile, not yet smooshed into formlessness, one can make out individual boards of lumber in dozens of different lengths and colors, the bright white of a drawer, a cardboard box with orange and green writing on its face.

This photograph is one of dozens captured by Ukeles's team during her eleven-month *Touch Sanitation Performance*, which started like many projects do, with a few observations, diagrams, and ideas scribbled on loose paper. On an early sheet of notes about the art of cleaning up, before *Touch Sanitation* was even conceived, Ukeles wrote, "Garbage is the ultimate mixed media." On another piece of paper, she drew a long, meandering line to represent how raw material becomes garbage. It was 1978, and she had just been named the first artist-in-residence at the Department of Sanitation for the City of New York (DSNY)—a position she herself created. She didn't know it then, but these first marks and notes would become a lifetime of making art with and out of garbage, and alongside garbage people.

o

I did not start making visual art until my early thirties. Prior to that, I wrote poems and short works of prose on my own and sometimes collaboratively with groups of friends. A few times each year, I would spend five dollars on a new sketchbook at the discount art supply place and attend a drop-in life drawing class. In college, I took the only two art classes available to non-majors. One provided basic painting instruction and the other some odd approaches—freehand embroidery among them—to drawing. Other than that, I had no training to speak of. I would never have called myself a writer, much less an artist.

During my twenties, I was busy with college, then striving to find a career that would pay my bills without making me want to walk into oncoming traffic, so making art was rarely a priority. But then one day, I found myself unemployed. The quest for a fulfilling, stable career had not panned out. I was broke, bored, and lonely during my long days alone at home while my partner worked. I cooked. I cleaned. I mended my favorite vintage shirts. I took out the garbage. When my chores were done, I thumbed through all the old magazines that he brought home from the barbershop attached to his office. I read them cover to cover, and then, instead of binding them with twine and tossing them into the recycling, I made something with them.

Around my house, I found scissors, electrical tape, junk mail, receipts, and glue sticks. I took a sheet of white paper and folded it into eights, then wrote little diary entries, random facts, bad dreams, and weird advice on the front side of each of the eight panels. I found that I liked making collages on the back side of the paper, a surprise that unfolded when the zine was spread flat. These were my first garbage works. I sent them to friends and family in the mail.

Next, I made huge collages on a big roll of drawing paper. For these, I cut out little circles and squares from larger images in magazines and newspapers, geometric fragments of gray guns, red mouths, dirty socks, polluted rivers, endangered birds, junk food and other cultural flotsam and jetsam. I placed the fragments on the huge paper with white space between them, creating sprawling constellations with unexpected connections.

Next, I made more collages, these ones smaller and more layered, often more direct in their messages about waste. I began photographing garbage around my neighborhood, and for a time, I folded these into my collage work. One piece from this period shows a diver's smooth, sculptural body plunging into a pile of empty plastic bottles, fast food wrappers, and laceless shoes. I was intimate with this particular pile; I spent time considering it every day, monitoring it for changes and additions, as I waited for my morning train. Another shows a man in lotus pose meditating on a filthy piece of cardboard.

A few months later, I abandoned the photographs in favor of garbage itself, which I am still figuring out how to work with. It is not easy to make garbage beautiful, but at least as I try to figure it out, I get closer and closer. I return to garbage, to wastelands and wasted lives, over and over again in my work, trying to make meaning from all the destruction. I do not always know why I am cutting up garbage and gluing it back together. I do know that my inspiration comes from many sources, and one is my personal struggle.

o

For her inaugural project with the DSNY, Ukeles decided on an ambitious durational performance. She set out to shake hands with every garbage man employed by the DSNY—all 8,500 of them. Many of these handshakes, like the one with the big-bellied man in beige, were photographed, I assume by an assistant. In each of them, Ukeles's tropical teal, bubblegum pink, and pastel blue work uniforms bloom like wildflowers in the dark fields of the garbage men's inky blacks and navy blues, against the backdrop of the dump's dusty browns.

In one photograph, Ukeles, this time wearing a more subdued forest green get-up, sits and talks with nine men in uniform. Cigarette butts line an ashtray in the middle of the table. A black object with buttons on top—a tape recorder?—stands next to the ashtray and an open pack of smokes. One man is on his feet, staring Ukeles dead in the eyes, wagging his finger in her face. She is looking at him intently, relaxed yet interested. I wonder what he is saying to her. I wonder if he is angry and, if so, what about.

I imagine he had plenty of complaints. In 1979, New York City teetered on the edge of bankruptcy and was, on the whole, coming undone. City employees were getting pink-slipped by the hundreds, sanitation workers were between strikes, and conditions in the DSNY garages were dismal. Ukeles says that these garages, which function as home-bases and break rooms for truck drivers, lacked even adequate toilets. The dilapidated, dim garages, with their stencil-painted signage and rows of metal lockers, stand out to me in the photographs of *Touch Sanitation* because they look so much like both public schools and prisons.

Another thing I notice in each of the photographs is Ukeles's head of well-coiffed, thick blonde hair, which she always wears gently styled, loose, and long. Her golden locks look almost gaudy next to the shaggy, grown-out do's of the sanitation men who chat with her at break room tables and in front of their trucks. Fluffy tufts of fuzz ring their shiny bald heads, mutton chops cushion their jawlines and obscure their ears, and wild strands fly in all directions from under their hats. Ukeles's blown-out hair and clean, bright outfits mark her as an outsider and make her hyper-visible. Her look smears artful, feminine beauty onto otherwise drab and dirty landscapes, much like a tag of red lipstick on a bar bathroom mirror. She is a looker. But could she get people to look at garbage as art?

o

The worst job I ever had was working as a maid. I cleaned houses for a national chain with franchise locations in many states. The company ran a permanent advertisement on Craigslist—a red flag, but I was not in a position to be picky. I was 17 years old when I walked into the cleaning service for a perfunctory interview, during which I was told that the job guaranteed minimum wage (then something like $7.15 per hour), but would often pay more, provided me and my team could clean fast enough.

This was not a job I wanted. I worked for the maid service because I was tired of fast food kitchens and too young for more desirable retail, restaurant, or childcare work. I also lacked connections that might've helped me get a better job. I had just moved to Portland from my rural hometown elsewhere in Oregon, and I had little to offer other than my young body and my willingness to get it dirty. I was hired on the spot.

The training videos were simple and directive. I watched them over several hours in the back of the cleaning service's office, which was really just a desk, a couple of folding tables with chairs, and some shelves in an otherwise empty commercial space. The cleaning women in the training videos had round bodies that they moved quickly and deliberately. They cut harsh, orderly lines into the vacuumed carpets. One woman wiped a mirror with a blue microfiber cloth, while the voice-over told me to shine any metallic fixture with glass cleaner so that it might gleam when the client later turned on the lights.

The women then demonstrated how to avoid leaving residue on the countertops or floors while also using the fewest number of rags. They taught me how to load and unload the car, deploy the vacuum, and scour a shower stall with minimal back strain. They showed how to clean an entire house using only a single bucket of water. Waste of cleaning products, the customer's time, or our labor (read: the cleaning company's profits) was a clear infraction. Of course, they also admonished me not to steal. The voice-over warned me to check each room for spray bottles, latex gloves, and stray scrub brushes before I left it. The only record of a maid having been in a house should be those touches of cleanliness—the shiny faucets, the carpet lines, the toilet paper's loose end folded into a neat triangle—the presence of our absence, a glaring lack of grime.

After training, I was given two ugly polo shirts. I signed a document saying that if I did not return the shirts, the cost of replacing them would be withheld from my final paycheck. Then, I was shown how to assemble a kit: the various cleaners, the gloves, the rags, the brushes, the garbage bags, a cloth apron.

I mostly worked with wizened older women who had been cleaning all of their lives. They reminded me of my maternal grandmother, Nana, who cleaned houses for a living. My mom also cleaned houses for a living—and cars and hotel rooms. My maternal great-grandmother was never a maid, but she cooked for many years at the local country club, feeding the people who made the down payments on the houses her daughter and granddaughter would later clean. Maybe it was inevitable that I, too, would end up cooking for and cleaning up after other people.

Sometimes, when I was still too small to babysit myself, Nana or Mom took me along on cleaning jobs. I grew up watching these women, the great loves of my life, scrub other people's toilets. I was not ashamed of my grandmother or my mother or of their work, but I was learning who we were in relation to other people.

I loved sitting in the wealthier kids' rooms while Nana and Mom cut harsh vacuum lines into the carpets and shined the fixtures. I admired the children's colorful, collectible toys carefully displayed on shelves like an exhibition of modernist sculptures. I could look, but I couldn't touch, and I didn't want to. I was content to admire, to be small, silent, and soft—a spy in a foreign land. It was there that I had first learned what to do at the end of a housekeeping shift. Our final disappearing act was to remove a garbage bag full of trash from the house, filled with all evidence of our having been there: expired food culled from fridges, haggard sponges, ammoniated newspaper, soiled paper towels stiff with dust and sweat.

At 17, and then, as the months dragged on, 18 years old, I rested my knees on cold linoleum, wiping pubic hairs and human waste from toilet bowls all over my city. One was always yellowed with dried urine—the older couple who lived there used an elevated seat which caused leaks and other accidents. I held my breath while I scrubbed at the calcified stains. I hated cleaning toilets, and I hated the cleaning company, who I knew was charging the client much more than was necessary and paying us less than we deserved while encouraging us to do quick, shoddy work that looked sparkling on the surface.

At least half of the houses, like the elevated toilet one, were truly gross. The other half looked completely unused. In one of these pristine houses in the suburban hills, a room between the living and dining rooms had been converted into an art gallery. A smooth white sculpture stood on a chest-high plinth a few feet from a large abstract oil painting in warm colors. A half dozen pieces in decorative frames adorned the other walls. Our instruction sheet for this house stated that the owners had this room specially cleaned by someone else. We were not to touch the art or even clean the floors. I glanced at the art for a few seconds, then tiptoed through the *verboten* space on my way to the bathroom where I knelt to wipe their toilet.

Rarely were clients home when we cleaned, and those who were seemed bashful. We all avoided eye contact. As we passed through their doorways with our dust rags and emptied their garbage cans, they said thank you from down the hall.

o

Garbage work, like most cleaning work, is unglamorous and difficult. Most people would rather not do it. They would rather not spend time reading about it, looking at it, studying it, or making art about it. But Ukeles looked, and she wanted others to look, too. She found it ridiculous that people could not or would not see the art of the work happening right in front of them.

To highlight the physical grace and efficiency of garbage collectors' daily exertions, Ukeles took her big hair and bright outfits out onto the streets where she shadowed garbage men on their routes, before and after their hand-shaking sessions. But she didn't just shadow them as in *tagged along*, she became the workers' technicolor shadow. As they collected trash from the streets, she mimed their movements. While they bent at the waist to grab bags from the sidewalks, she bent at the waist. When they swung a bag up into the back of the truck, she swung her imaginary bag. When they heaved, she heaved, turning the act of garbage collection into a dance. Many years later, Ukeles expanded on this practice when she choreographed her work ballets. These dances were performed by laborers and their work machines. Documentation of these ballets shows a tugboat nuzzling a barge, lines of trucks snaking along a waterway in perfect formation, and two snow plows engaged in a duet, their metal noses dipping up and down as they reach out to touch.

o

To accomplish the feat of shaking the hands of 8,500 sanitation workers, Ukeles created detailed maps that coincided with the Department's routes and day/night shift work schedules. She called her routes "sweeps." In addition to shaking hands and mimicking the workers's movements on these sweeps, Ukeles interviewed the men. She also delivered speeches about her own work and the value of theirs at beginning-of-shift roll calls at the garages. She spent either eight or sixteen hours sweeping each day, traveling the city with all the people who take our garbage away. Ukeles told the men she was not there to study or analyze them, but rather to be with them, to witness the as-yet-unwitnessed art they were making.

Her inspiration for the performance came from many sources, and one was her personal struggle. She had been working hard to create a thriving art career during the 1960s and 70s while also doing the unpaid and often tedious job of being a mother—a job she came to consider its own sort of art. "I do a hell of a lot of washing, cleaning, cooking, renewing, supporting, preserving etc." Ukeles wrote in her 1969 "Maintenance Art Manifesto." "I also 'do' art. Now, I will simply do these maintenance everyday things and flush them up to consciousness, exhibit them, as Art." She decided to see her work in a new way and began to propose works that made public the activity of caring, cleaning, and repairing. As to a description of what constitutes art under her rubric, Ukeles writes, "Everything I say is Art is Art. Everything I do is Art is Art."

A fascination with cleaning and maintenance work at home led Ukeles to think about entire systems of maintenance. In her manifesto, she noted that "the culture confers lousy status on maintenance jobs = minimum wages, housewives = no pay," an ideology she continued to make visible and resist through her art practice. A decade later, with her touch performance, she hoped to trouble popular misconceptions about garbage workers' contributions and intelligence, just as she had done in prior works of Maintenance Art. From a list of commands under her definition of Art come the following: clean your desk, clean the floor, change the baby's diaper, fix the typos, and "throw out the stinking garbage." As a mother, she felt a kinship with garbage men whom she called "the housekeepers of the city."

The goal of Ukeles's' hand-shaking project was to go and say thanks—to learn about the people who did the dirty, invisible maintenance of cleaning up our cities. She was sure that hundreds of people would join in on the performance, forming a parade of gratitude that would coalesce alongside her as she followed the DSNY trucks. People did not come, to Ukeles's surprise, but occasionally someone would stop to watch as she followed along with the workers. Others parted the blinds to stare from their darkened windows.

Ukeles has now been the artist-in-residence at DSNY for over forty years. Hers is an unpaid position.

o

Looking at and touching what's trashed, then, is radical. I want people to see what I see, even when it is scary, stinky, sad, and awful. I also want people to consider that there is more than one way of seeing and that you'll never see without looking. Like Ukeles, I am touching, and I am looking. I am asking questions such as, *What if instead of discarding, we drew near? What if instead of bagging or burying, we laid bare?*

Recently, I have zoomed in to focus my artwork on the garbage inside my house. I save tin foil, shipping envelopes, various boxes, bubble wrap, price tags, paper sleeves, and colorful nets that once held mandarins or avocados. While I handle these materials, I try to discern what is inside of them, beyond the essential roughness of their cardboard flaps and the stickiness of their plastic bubbles. I feel for the original, raw materials before they were harvested or mined, melted or molded, chopped or dyed. I appreciate their bold colors, and I imagine the faces of the people who labored in factories to make them. I arrange these materials into collages and flat sculptures trying to make something beautiful of all the work that went into them. I also incorporate my garbage into my found-image collages. Sometimes, I even make photocopies of my trash. I do not yet know why I do this, but I think it has something to do with appreciation. Sometimes it feels like a seance.

Garbage becomes art when someone reconsiders it as not-useless, not-dead, or not-void, which is to say valuable, worthy, and deserving of reverence. As a material with a message. Through an artist's deliberate gaze, salvaged materials, trashy lives, and dirty work can become more, can become representational or symbolic, and can bring bounty where there once was lack. The throw-away becomes the held-close, the altarpiece, the heirloom, the dance. Garbage becomes art through the quality of our attention. Or, as a friend said, "Trash is an adjective."

Maybe this is why I am making garbage art—to try to imagine a different context, a different set of definitions. I am constructing a world in which nothing and no one is wasted, at least without a proper eulogy. If we pause to consider what we are throwing away before we trash it, perhaps we will know when to stop.

o

I was not thinking about toilets when I walked into the 2021 Greater New York exhibition at MoMa PS1; I was thinking about art and care. In the first room I entered, I found 366 tiny trash sculptures, each constructed inside of the crispy cellophane rectangle from a discarded cigarette pack. The artist had arrayed them in acrylic boxes like days on a calendar, seven slots by five in each of 12 containers that hung on the wall. From the way the delicate materials were placed with clear attention to each fold and bend, each texture and hue, I could tell that the artist cared deeply about this garbage. "[Yuji] Agematsu arranges bits of refuse so delicately," wrote one reviewer, "that a bent Q tip hovering above a pool of melted lollipop looks more like ikebana than abject filth." Devotion pulsed through the clear container and seemed to suspend the sculptures in just the right positions.

Agematsu began making these pieces in 1980 when he moved to the US from Japan. On his daily walks around New York City, he gathered small pieces of trash from the sidewalks he traversed. The debris he collected—the feathers, thread, spit-out gum, washers, hair nets, receipts, feathers, foil, and fake flowers—became a tangible record of a particular path on a particular day. He also annotated these paths in tiny composition books, recording his material entanglement with others who had walked those same sidewalks, leaving their detritus behind. The concept was cool, but I stayed for its beauty.

Shards of colorful glass leaned against brilliant reflective candy wrappers. Green wads of gum stacked on blue wads of gum stacked on red wads of gum wore a little wig of straw-like twine. A ketchup packet, a broken crayon, a sharp metal something, and an ashy matchstick engaged in an affair. A silky ribbon and several purple flowers cradled a baby bird's skeleton. Looking at these sculptures, I was overcome by the suggestion of something hidden among these details of our lives and the threads of connection they held to the people who owned them, broke them, used them, and lost them. These people rode the subway, smoked cigarettes, bought lottery tickets, and had bad breath. People like me and maybe like you. Here was the real stuff of life, the profane and the refuse, in a box on a wall.

If I were going to make something for this exhibition, I would buy a car from the junkyard off HWY 99 that we passed driving to my late grandparents' house. I would take that car—an old, heavy model—smashed up and partially parted out and display it as a sculpture on a rectangle of astroturf with potted dandelions and blackberry bushes around it. Next to that I could install a washing machine with broken knobs, a cracked hose, and rust creeping along its seams in an abstract pattern, the corroded lines like blood in its veins. Over there I could hang a rack of decaying clothes to show what breaks down and what doesn't (a pair of skinny jeans turns to rubber bands after a short time in the elements). Over there, I could install a landfill core sample in a glass tube. Next to that, an arcade claw game filled with broken toys. My crown jewel might be a collection of trash assemblages representing profiles from different zip codes, exemplifying how an average person lives there and what they can afford to throw away. I could put them in plexiglass boxes and hang them on the wall.

o

Where I grew up, folk artists, mostly aging hippies with thinning ponytails and Jesus-like leather sandals, made a lot of art out of garbage. They were fervent environmentalists and their work constituted a material representation of their political lives. They tie-dyed "Give Peace A Chance" t-shirts by the dozen and wore them to the Saturday Market, where their fellow craftspeople sold handmade patchwork tote bags, watercolor greeting cards, and black rubber belts made from salvaged bike tubes.

Across the river, on the less liberal side of town, a car repair shop at the intersection of 28th and Main Streets sold planters made from disused truck tires, their flayed tips accented with fluorescent spray paint. We passed these planters on the way to and from everywhere, and each time I rolled my eyes. Further out on the edges of town, scarecrows with hubcap heads and hand-me-down clothes guarded the rows of small farms. Art was everywhere. I called it garbage.

I hated all of these working-class artworks, especially the spray-painted tire planters. I loathed the way they flaunted their junkiness and felt embarrassed by how easy it was to work them into punchlines. I pitied the makers for their ignorance at not just pointing out their poverty, but highlighting it in neon pink paint. I couldn't see their work for what it was—an expression of humanity, an ecstatic gesture. Instead, I smeared them with the trash of my adjectives.

I never recognized any of this as art because nobody named it as such. Art happened in great cities like New York, long ago or far away. It sat arrayed in royal tombs and adorned the ceilings of Renaissance chapels. Art decorated the walls in wealthy people's houses. Art classes were not available to me in middle or high school, and nobody encouraged me to write nor make visual art. I was told I would make a great English teacher or a good Spanish-English translator. Perhaps I could even work for the US government. I was the daughter of working-class people who didn't think art was for them, and who didn't know about women like Ukeles and her "Maintenance Art Manifesto." Creative pursuits were an afterthought, as in, after the work day is done, the bills are paid, the kids are fed, and the toilets are clean. It took me a long time—almost thirty years—to admit that I was an artist. It took me that long to see it.

o

In 1979, Mierle Laderman Ukeles stood on several tons of compacted trash. A worker had just dumped the load from his truck. Following her custom, Ukeles walked up to him and shook his hand, thanking him for keeping New York City alive. He thanked her with a story: He and his crew had been out picking up garbage on a humid, 90-degree day in Brooklyn. After loading up the trash in front of one house, the workers sat on its stoop, taking a moment to rest. A woman came out of the house and shouted them away. "Get away from here," she snarled at the sanitation workers, "I don't want you smelling up my porch."

The worker expressed great relief at being seen and heard by Ukeles, by having his suffering witnessed. He begged her to remember his story and to tell it to anyone who might benefit from a warning against such ridicule. As a monument to this worker's suffering, Ukeles rebuilt the front porch from the story at the entrance to the Ronald Feldman gallery in SoHo. She then asked the sanitation department to compile lists of the worst names their workers had been called. She collected a long list of epithets. Next, Ukeles and her team painted the names in bright primary colors onto the glass-and-wood installation. She invited 190 people, including sanitation workers, to come and wash the offending nouns and adjectives away. These names, of which there were dozens, included:

Scum grummer
Dirtbag
Pig
Slime ball
Flunkie douche rag
Maggot
Low-life doing low-life work
Shithead
Scumbag

As the words were washed away, people cried and cheered.

"Do you call yourself a garbage person?" Ukeles asked civilians who turned up their noses at her work with DSNY. "*You're* the one who made the garbage; it's not their garbage." People thought garbage was gross, and they did not want to be associated with it, not even with its removal, not even when it was they who made the mess. They especially did not think that garbage could be art.

o

I cannot remember being called demeaning names when I was young, nor, for that matter, as an adult. What I do remember is overhearing small town gossip. People who looked and talked and acted like me and my family were called—and called each other—the following:

Broke-ass
White trash
Dirty kid
Ghetto
Welfare case
Tweaker
Trailer trash

Mostly, though, there were subtler messages. I remember my teachers, each of them well-meaning I'm sure, who warned us about bleak futures working at McDonald's or the gas station when we were misbehaving. My parents didn't do these jobs exactly, but they spent their days doing maintenance work. I worked night shifts at Taco Bell, feeding people dinner. I scrubbed crusty beans from metal cambro containers and squirted orange cheese goo onto the tortilla chips I had fried. What, I wondered, did these teachers think they were accomplishing, threatening us with our very own lives?

I always wanted to go to college, and everyone knew that I would, including my teachers, even the ones who made me feel bad about myself inadvertently. I was encouraged to get a degree so that I could be better than my parents. Was it *be better* or *have more*? They sounded the same to me.

The name *garbage man* has fallen out of vogue since the '70s, though it is certainly still used. The gentler, more accurate *sanitation worker* is now the more common term, a shift that matters a lot to Ukeles and, in a way, to me. What we call ourselves and what we hear others call us teaches us who we are. Try as we might to resist the names hurled at us, we hear how we are spoken about. Eventually, we come when we are called, even if it hurts.

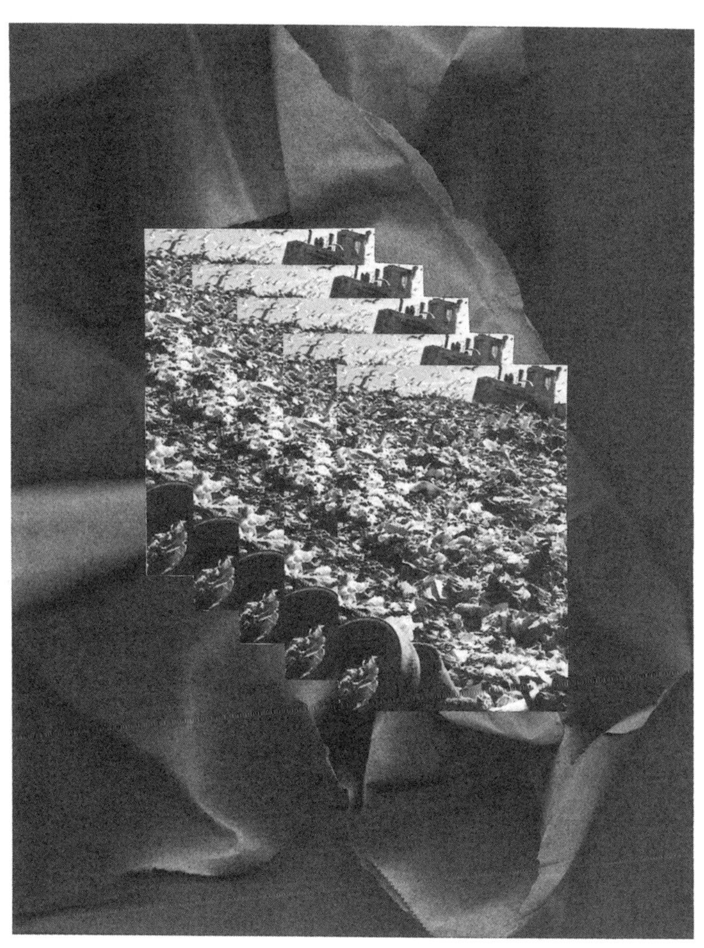

RITUALS TO SEE TRASH #3

1. Move to a rural area where there is no municipal garbage service. As the refuse of your daily life accumulates, do not take your trash to the dump. Instead, use bags of it to create a sculpture garden near your home.

2. When the sculpture garden becomes too large and begins to crowd you out of your space, document it as an Earthwork.

3. Acquire a burn barrel.

4. Sort your garbage by color and material. Once sorted, burn each heap in the barrel. Notice what disappears and what doesn't. Invite your neighbors to partake in this ritual. Document this as a piece of performance art.

5. Gather the ashes from your barrels. Mix the ashes with water and use them to create paintings that are political in nature. Show the paintings in a gallery funded by profits from fracking.

6. Send the garbage that remains—what wouldn't burn—back to its manufacturer. Apply for an arts grant to cover shipping and handling. Document this, too, as a performance.

ART UNDER DURESS

It was a time when I needed color the most.

I have always tended toward melancholy. That year had been particularly difficult. In spring, I felt immaterial, but my work kept me tethered to the living. I got on the train and then stood in front of classrooms of expectant students, pretending to be a professor. The act drained me of my vigor, and my sorrow was unremitting. By summer, I cried indiscriminately and at the slightest provocation. The J train, a friend's birthday party, my thesis reading, the backseat of a taxi, the laundromat: I wept at all of them. I had hoped for a kaleidoscopic year of vivid experience. Reality was much paler or, when colored, more gruesome.

In August, I tripped on a step going down into the subway at 68th Street. All I saw were the fluorescent lights and my grimy white shoes as I fell toward the oily, black-pocked floor. When I caught myself with my right hand, I knew the result would be violent. My bruises were green and black blooms. They were yellow and purple. They were blue.

At the doctor's office, they said I was overreacting. But I'm an artist, I said. I'm a writer. I need my hands. I felt crazy.

Because I was on Medicaid, I had to go to Bellevue, a public hospital, to see about my bones, some of which were fractured. Days—then weeks—after the fall, my pointer finger still looked like a bloated, blue sausage. My palm stayed tender. Again, the doctors rolled their eyes at me. They told me to buy a splint at the drugstore and to look up physical therapy exercises on the internet.

Outside Bellevue, in front of the psych ward, I watched a girl in gray grippy socks and a gray sweat-suit drag on a cigarette, her gray-hooded head lost in a cloud of gray smoke. I looked up at the brick wall of the hospital and considered checking myself in, as I had many times before, but I was sure that being drugged into oblivion on a strange white bed in a gray-walled room would not cure me. A state-funded mental hospital wouldn't be much different from the cells I had seen in jails for children or in drug and alcohol diversion units. I had my own room like that at home, and it was hardly salutary.

o

From his gray universe at Indiana State Prison, Etheridge Knight wrote a poem entitled "Cell Song," which reads: "Night Music Slanted / Light strike the cave of sleep. I alone / tread the red circle / and twist the space with speech…/ can there anything / good come out of / Prison." The red circle lends itself to speculation. Is Knight chewing on a circular, angry thought? Is the red circle the slanted light of a blood moon on the floor? I wish it were a dream shape, but most likely, the circle is literal, a penal demarcation. Perhaps he was circling danger, toeing the threshold while talking to himself, painting a poem with his mouth across the shadowy, institutional night.

In 1960, Knight landed in prison on a robbery charge after a shrapnel injury in the Korean War led to a drug addiction. By then, he had mastered the popular African American art of "toasts"—public performances of rhymed epic poems—that vivified drug deals, hot nights, fist fights, and other heroic adventures. Like many toasters, Knight deployed the specialized language of the streets in his recitations, including slang, obscenities, and the clever abuse of double and triple entendre—what polite society might call *colorful language*. His acumen translated perfectly to written poems.

While incarcerated, Knight recorded what he saw both inside and on television, shaping his emotive analyses into poems that experimented with established forms. He used pastoral imagery and made political references, but charged his lines with dialogue that he heard on his cell block or out on the yard. The result was his signature style—a melange of opposites that melded high art with low.

As is common among inmate populations, Knight wasn't a scholar of literature or art, and he didn't hail from a well-connected family. He was a member of the trashed classes, made doubly trash by his status as prisoner, and his art was destined to remain obscure, particularly because it railed against the brutality he and his fellow lowlives endured. He made work anyway. "Poetry and a few people in there trying to stay human saved me," he said. "I knew that I couldn't just deaden all my feeling the way some people did."

During his sentence, Knight published his first poem in the mainstream magazine *Negro Digest*, later renamed *Black World*, and began corresponding with acclaimed African American writers of the period. His early success was unusual for an artist working behind bars. Work by imprisoned artists is generally derided or ignored by cultural institutions, and

Knight's mail was censored by the prison in an attempt to thwart further publication, but he continued to write and smuggle out work through friends. Stars like Gwendolyn Brooks and Dudley Randall visited him inside, and Knight swiftly became part of the Black Arts Movement. His skill and connections carried him to well-deserved acclaim.

Knight ultimately produced *Poems from Prison*, his first of several collections, which was published in 1968, the same year he completed his sentence. This collection, which I discovered by happenstance during grad school (it wasn't on the syllabus), illuminates the ragged emotional terrain of remaining human—a being that laughs, rages, creates, fucks, fights, lives, and thinks—amid difficult, degrading conditions.

Although trapped inside the achromatic world of the penitentiary, Knight's poems seethe color. Sunset. Yellow eyes. The blues. Brown hill. Split purple lips. Plum. Star bright ice. Inmates lounging like lizards on rocks. Terrible portraits of knives and drunks rendered in a brilliant palette.

o

I became fascinated by prison art during childhood when my uncle came home from a stint inside and began airbrushing t-shirts. He set up his system—a pen-sized silver gun with a black hose that attached to a compressor, some inks, and a tarp—on the concrete slab porch behind my grandparents' house. Onto white blanks, he sprayed vibrant pink and orange roses, blue dolphins in aquamarine waters, and simple words in graffiti-style letters. I observed from a distance as the clouds of ink formed into recognizable shapes on the cloth. As I remember it, he had learned to airbrush in prison, which deeply confused me. When I had made a birthday card to send to him the year prior, before his release, my grandma had denied my request for markers or crayons. Colored pencil only, she had said, handing me a few permitted colors. Everything else is against the rules. If he couldn't have a piece of paper with marker on it, how could he have had the gun, the inks, and the shirts? My grandmother is gone, and I am estranged from my uncle, so I won't attempt to find the answer to this question. It doesn't matter anyway. The significance of this memory is that it predicts a life interested in low art, an intimacy with the carceral state, and an obsession with the ways people use color to conjure meaning from the abyss.

o

As summer became fall and then winter, I said goodbye to two lovers, my profession, a friend, an apartment, and a city. I went to bed with my crying, and I didn't get out. I knew I was pathetic, but neither that knowledge nor the shame it brought me made any difference.

He moved out and took everything with him: the bed, the couch, the desk, the tv, the air conditioner, the popcorn bowl, the blender. All I had left was my thin mattress on the floor and a few boxes of black and white books. My world was an eight-by-twelve-foot room, white walls, white sheets, white pillowcases, white curtains, and a gray-black linen blanket.

Yet I must admit that I had told him to take everything. I felt lighter knowing I wouldn't have possessions to worry about. I was preparing for something, but I didn't know what. Maybe to die. Not dramatically, but by simply fading out.

It felt like the world's slowest emergency. I needed a supernatural intervention, someone to breathe color back into my face. I was bloodless. The thought of guardian angels visited and stayed. I'd always thought the concept corny, but this time it gave me solace.

Of course, I got up periodically. The semester kept starting. I had to go teach. In my best moments, I began thinking I could make work again. From bed, I ordered magazines, mostly ones about birds. Because of the angels, I was thinking about spirits, about freedom and flight.

My materials came in the mail. The birding magazines held huge washes of cerulean sky and azure water on their pages. Otherwise, they were a flurry of brown and gray feathers. I stood at my table and cut wings, faces, gargoyles' heads, penises, ballet skirts, branches, breasts, fragments of ancient sculptures, stones. On tiles of white porcelain—inexpensive, practical, and reminiscent of the knick-knacks that comprised the majority of the art to which I was exposed during my provincial childhood—I began to assemble my angels. Their colors were soft. Lilac-gray, green-gray, gray-pink. Brown and blue. They looked as if they were being resuscitated, or as if they were monuments in the process of coming to life.

But then there were other images that would not leave me. The white-walled houses of my youth.

The white rectangle of my bed. Waiting rooms like caves of ice.

o

What if I told you that what I remember most was his color? His skin was the greasy gray of the sidewalks in New York City. This was during his first prison sentence, when he was still just a boy—nineteen, twenty, then twenty-one. My brother had long been a lawbreaker, and consequently, he was broken by the law. He had seen many gray rooms.

When he walked across the beige-tiled floor and sat down at the table in the visiting room at a medium-security prison in Eastern Oregon, the first thing I noticed was his utter lack of luster. My family and I were there to see him for the last time before his release, just weeks away. We hugged and sat around the table. I asked him what was wrong.

"When they know your date's coming up, they can get jealous and wanna start shit," my brother said about his fellow inmates. His tawny hair was thinning and he had the skittish, sickly disposition of a lab rat. The stresses of institutional life—the bad work, politics, and boredom—were wearing him down, aging him in fast-forward.

He explained that it was safer to stay in his cell than to continue with his regular schedule of eating in the mess hall, exercising on the yard, and doing grunt work around the campus where he cleaned the bathrooms and took out the trash. For nourishment, he survived on what he could buy from the commissary and prepare in his cell or by using the on-tier microwave. This amounted mostly to foods in the brown-yellow color family, that of the cheap corn and wheat that comprised their scientifically-produced ingredients: packets of mush, ramen noodles, bitter instant coffee, and Little Debbie snacks. He spent his days close to his cot, doing push-ups and minding his own business. When we picked him up in the family van on the freezing winter morning that marked the end of his sentence, he was as thin and gray as the off-brand instant oatmeal on which he had been subsisting. He had nearly wasted away.

Years later, as an inmate at another site of the Oregon Department of Corrections, my brother wore a standard issue uniform: blue jeans, blue work shirt, white socks, and one of four sneaker options sold by the commissary. Emblazoned over the knees, heart, and upper back of his outfit were neon orange DOC insignia. "Why do they have those logos on there?" I once asked. "What do they think, you're gonna steal the clothes?" I laughed at the absurdity of taking home the prison's uniform, imagining a now-free man in full jail dress walking through the cruel streets of the city, homesick for his small, hard cell.

"They're targets," my brother replied. "So that they can shoot you from far off."

In the winter of my depression, I taught a creative writing residency at a school for children in non-secure detention, meaning they were somewhere between home and jail or between jail and home. One wrote a poem that reminded me of Knight's cell song, with its maddening solitude and search for meaning amid the meaningless hours. My student wrote, "The eeriness of silence. / Furious yet so still. / I think I'm going crazy. / Isolated in a population… / Faced with decisions. / Chow? Rec? Or life and death."

At the school, kids were herded around on a careful schedule based on the colors of their shirts, which were navy, black, hunter green, and maroon. Their writing conjured a world smeared with blood red and television blue, a world of black dogs and Christmas presents wrapped in gold foil. My own work paled in comparison.

o

Constraints on time and space may be the most salient markers of captivity, but what about color?

Jails and prisons are fortresses of gray. Their cinder block walls are painted in pasty neutrals, pallid pastels, or, more rarely, white. Everything is made of cool, hard materials, all colored in gloomy shades. Yet, on closer inspection, a prison is not devoid of color at all. It is a place where color rules. In this case, I'm not talking about gangs or racial inequality, though both are of great consequence. I'm talking about paint and dye and pigment. I'm talking about art.

Nicole Fleetwood calls the colors of the institution "penal hues." In her book *Marking Time*, a breathtaking survey of modern art created within carceral spaces, she explains the significance of color against the largely muted, lifeless palette of the broader institutional space. Orange, for one, is a "stress color" because of its associations with areas forbidden to prisoners, a color line that is enforced with violence. Orange can also be anxiety-provoking because of its common use for jailhouse clothing, a choice that makes inmates hypervisible and easily surveilled—or, as with my brother's clothes, shot at—against the gray-white of the mess hall or the blacktop of the yard. Clothing colors, like floor markings, can also carry a code; they separate minimum from maximum security prisoners and inmates from both staff and visitors. In an adult prison, a child sometimes wears a different color from his fellows, a choice that both protects and endangers him.

For me, the most interesting parts of Fleetwood's book are those that detail artists' rebellions against restriction. Tight controls on what can enter the facility from the outside limit incarcerated artists' work. Vibrant red and blue pigments, for example, can contain metallic or flammable materials that aren't allowed in prisons, and absent special programs, artists can get only a few supplies from the commissary—the prison store—if they have funds from working or from loved ones. In the absence of color, incarcerated artists create dyes from makeup, magazines, hair products, tea, coffee, candy made with artificial coloring, shoe polish, or even Kool Aid.

Ndume Olatushani, a man wrongfully convicted of murder who spent twenty years on death row in Tennessee before he was released, turned to color as a freedom practice during his confinement. Olatushani drapes his figures in a jewel box of rich, dynamic colors and positions them in verdant, borderless environments. In the repressive climate of death row, "The one thing people couldn't control was my mind and my thoughts," he said to Fleetwood. "I refused to give that up… Even though you've got me in this colorless environment, you can't stop the color that was actually happening in my head."

o

While my brother was incarcerated, we could only send in books or magazines through approved third-party retailers, and he wrote us letters on plain lined paper using stubby, eraserless pencils. The Department of Corrections prohibited care packages of any sort, so even if he had wanted art supplies, which he never asked for or mentioned, we couldn't have sent them. Still, I believe that if he had wanted to make art, he would have found a way. Despite everything I have seen, or maybe because of it, I have faith in that kind of ingenuity and endurance.

Maybe finding a way was what I was doing with my collages. I wasn't sure that art could do anything for me, and yet there I was making it out of whatever was available: trash magazines, old library books, other people's art, the kindness of strangers and friends. It wasn't a compulsion, and it wasn't a hobby or a therapy. It was a revolt—against grief, against meaninglessness, against silence. It was a refusal to lay down and die.

o

Though I was the most depressed I had ever been, the angels came out of my hands. As they accumulated on my desk and, when I ran out of room, on the floor, I noticed that they were a sorrowful family. Looking to other artists for inspiration, some of them incarcerated, I wondered if I should make an effort to be more vibrant. I combed through the magazines and books again, clipping out more colorful cuttings. I didn't like the bright collages as much, and I didn't understand why. I decided it was my lack of skill. I hoped that if I studied color more, I could master its use, that somehow color could make my work more profound or (forgive me) arresting. At some point in this pursuit, I had to ask myself, What is color? As if a definition was ever enough. As if by describing a thing, we know it.

I tried to know color anyway. I read that it is the result of electromagnetic radiation, little waves and particles that bounce around inside my eye sockets and which my brain interprets as yellow or purple or pink. I had always known that color is related to light, that there is a spectrum—a rainbow—produced by a prism, but I still found it interesting that while a person can see shapes in dim light, colors appear only when more light is present. I wonder if this has any relationship to the way that during a period of dark depression, one feels life has been leached of its color. Similarly, I wonder if the brain ever mistakes a flatly colored visual field, such as a gray room with gray metal furniture, for darkness.

Finding oneself cornered, it helps to have something greater to believe in. Facing a war, the loss of a loved one, or some other personal crisis—like a prison sentence—many turn toward the divine for hope and salvation. So what would happen if I turned to color?

o

I asked my friend, a classically trained painter, to teach me how to make colors. We sat on her green velvet couch, and she swirled brushes through the pigment-rich rectangles of her watercolor set to make tints of brown and blue, skin and sky. I took notes while I watched and listened.

"I have a color in my head," I said, "but I can't make it come out." It was that of dune grass against a smear of gray clouds. This led to a discussion of color as a product of relationship and context. Colors, like people and the things they make, are attributed value in relationship to one another—light and dark, high and low.

Then another friend told me about *Werner's Nomenclature of Color*. I had never heard of it. The nomenclature is a reference book, a taxonomy of 108 colors, each entry consisting of a sample swatch, natural comparisons, and brief compositional description. Dutch Orange, for example, which resembles prison jumpsuits, is described as a mixture of "gamboge yellow with carmine red," matching the "Crest of Golden crested Wren" and the "Common Marigold."

In the early 1800s, Scottish botanical painter Patrick Syme picked up the nomenclature where Abraham Gottleb Werner, an 18th century geologist, had left off years prior ("Born into a mining family, Werner was surrounded by rocks throughout his childhood"—how someone can take a hard, gray vocation and make it colorful). Syme, scholar of plants and their colors, acknowledged that hues were often misidentified, not to mention too various to account for in their sum total, and that some structure needed to be brought to bear on this madness in order to properly describe, and thus know, the world. "How defective, therefore, must description be when the terms used are ambiguous; and where there is no regular standard to refer to," Syme complained. As a remedy, he aimed to clarify the names of colors, and establish a standard rubric for identifying them. Thumbing through the book, I found myself running my finger over each box of color. Maybe I thought I could come to know color carnally.

"In describing an object, to specify its colors is always useful," Syme wrote, "but where color forms a character, it becomes absolutely necessary." In a world without photography, Syme felt that describing shapes and dimensions was inadequate. Color was imperative.

To grasp this, I imagined a cell, a small room with only a bunk bed and a combination toilet-sink. Then I added that the cell measured six by eight feet and housed two people, each between five and six feet tall, further clarifying the image. Then I colored the walls a dim, nauseated green (matching most closely Werner's Asparagus Green, color of the brimstone butterfly), the toilet stainless steel, the floor a swirling gray, a concrete sky verging on rain. I saw his point.

The *Nomenclature* was recently re-released as a slim volume bound in cloth the color of a robin's egg, a hue Werner might call Verditer Blue. My favorite color description in the book is that of Skimmed-milk White, identified as "the white of the human eyeball," its juxtaposition of milk and eye visceral and grisly.

Months later, still working on my angels, still tormented by the idea of hue and my inability to reproduce it from my mind's eye accurately, I made a color wheel from yellow, blue, and red paint. It was shockingly difficult and took me hours to complete. The muddled greens and purples revealed my ineptitude, but my oranges turned out, somehow, perfect.

The only thing I learned from all this is that color is a kind of light.

o

I am not trying to equate depression with incarceration, though feeling trapped inside one's mind makes for an easy metaphor. I do find it interesting that while depressed, memories of my brother's confinement and my interactions with the institution surfaced over and over. Weakened by my illness, I had little power to fight off thoughts and feelings that I could usually keep on the periphery of my consciousness. Perhaps this was my psyche's perverse way of nudging me toward the light, the way some people say, *Well, it could always be worse,* referencing war-torn nations and starving children in response to the revelation of a more mundane difficulty.

I am trying to say something about power and inspiration, about the ways color and survival and freedom interrelate. I am trying to say something about regaining control of one's life.

o

From her Egyptian prison cell, the artist Inji Efflatoun wrote, "I still paint a lot, with determination and inspiration; the subjects are always the same but with a new vision, a purer and more sober vision; for me, it's about constantly renewing myself in this world of the unrenewable." Efflatoun painted dozens of bold, iterative portraits of the women with her in prison. Her subjects' expressions are by turns icy and incandescent, mournful and dreamy, composed of thick lines and triangles in eggplant, saffron, scarlet, and chestnut. These portraits repeat content but with small shifts in style and color, which mark the passage of time and Efflatoun's changing perspective. In addition to portraits, she painted a tree outside her cell over and over—first in red, then pink, then brown, then blue—as if tracing the curves of its branches would transport her outside the bars and into a landscape of liberation. I wonder if it worked, if while she was painting her tree she went somewhere else, as I did while making my angels.

Unlike most American detainees, Efflatoun was not in on a drug, theft, or parole violation. She was a political prisoner locked up by the dictatorship for her intellectual and Communist affiliations. While incarcerated, she was allowed to paint sporadically. At first, the prison allowed her to work, but stipulated that any finished pieces could be sold by the prison's leadership. Some of her works went to prison employees, others were confiscated, and surely others were bought by art collectors or laypeople. Because of this, it's difficult to know the true scope of her work, though fifty or so pieces from this period survive.

The similarities between Efflatoun's situation and those of modern prison artists in the US are striking. All suffer the whims and restrictions of the institution. Following my brother's journey through the prisons, I learned that inmates are moved constantly, but at the same time are severely limited in terms of who and what they see. Inmates must also abide by controls on how much property they can keep, generally as much as will fit in a small locker. Excess or suspect material can be confiscated without warning. Even, my brother told me, a piece of garbage, like an empty food container, could promote ingenuity and thus threaten "the safety and security of the facility" (I hated hearing him talk like that).

In fall and then winter and then spring, I tried to make other work. I tried to write. I couldn't. The only work I could do was on the angels, one after the other, or six at once, mimetic manifestations of a subconscious obsession I was developing with divine intervention. After days-long stints where I could do nothing but cry and lie in my bed, I goaded myself on with stories like Efflatoun's. People have made art under much more difficult conditions, I told myself, including in hospitals, mental institutions, and prisons. Surely I could make some in my room.

o

Then the police came for my mother. She was arrested. If I said it was a case of identity theft, would you believe me? It doesn't matter. The story is colorful, regardless.

She was taken on the side of the road. It was green out, an early summer evening. She was wearing her work clothes: black pants and a short-sleeved floral print blouse. The warrant showed her name, but a stranger's birthday. Oh, well. Our family is known to the police—many of us have criminal records for this or that crime of poverty—so it was pointless to argue, though she tried. My niece, eight years old, watched the lights tint the world red and blue from the passenger seat. Just out of view, the officer cuffed Mom. He took her to jail.

When she stepped out of the car into the gated parking lot, hands wreathed in silver behind her back, she was told to stand on the red line. When the door opens, walk through it and go to the left, the officer said. She did as she was told.

Inside and to the left, a silent, invisible camera snapped her picture. Tattoos? She turned to show the pink and purple hearts on her arm—a piece done by her brother, my uncle, the airbrusher, who had also learned to tattoo in prison—each inscribed in black with the first initial of one of her children.

After booking, she was told to stand at the next red line, wait for the door to open, then go through and face the blue wall. The doors were heavy steel with thick glass windows and their clanging echoed as they closed behind her. An officer frisked her: under her boobs, in her ass crack, crotch to foot. Take off your shoes, the corrections officer said. Five feet away, a red X marked a spot on a bench. The CO directed her there, then took her shoes and gave her orange slippers.

Then it was time to enter holding or, as it is called colloquially, the fishbowl. A CO explained the rules. Mom had been there twenty years earlier, in another lifetime, but she hadn't forgotten them. Windows covered one wall so that the COs—mostly doing nothing at their desks, Mom said later—could surveil the holding pen with little effort. Don't look through the windows. Don't stand at the windows. Over there is a piece of red tape. If you have a question, you stand on the tape with your back to the door and wait for an officer to call you. The CO continued with a litany of color-coded rules.

Before leaving her alone in the fishbowl (it was a quiet evening), the CO handed Mom a white styrofoam container. Like if you're in the hospital, Mom said. Or a mental institution, I thought. Inside the container was a cardboard spoon soggy with green bean juice. Mom was starving. *Fuck it I'll use my fingers*, she thought, and dug them into a mound of yellow macaroni and cheese which was, she had to admit, really good. Between bites, she identified hotdog-colored meat flecks among the noodles and flicked them to the side.

Time passed. She filled her paper cup from the tiny gray sink in the bathroom with no door. Nobody called her to sit on the blue stool in the corner to discuss the details of her detention. She shivered and watched the silent TV mounted inside a metal cage high up on the wall. After a few more hours and several phone calls, punctuated briefly by a woman, high on speed or otherwise manic, who would not stop talking, she made bail for $840, supplied by my brother, now paroled and working as a truck driver.

The color game played in reverse. Red lines, blue walls, orange slippers. Her shoes, phone, and wallet in a clear plastic bag. They gave her two white papers—a bail receipt and a court date. Three weeks later, the charges were dismissed. The bail money was returned, less fees. She did not lose her job or spend a single night in a cell. Still, her heart races at red and blue lights in the rearview mirror or sweeping across the front lawn.

o

In the violently green exam room at the community clinic where I receive primary care from medical students, I am diagnosed with a common depressive disorder. I am given purple pills to take and am surprised when they work. They don't erase my despair completely, but they give me what my mother calls "a pep in my step." She is on the purple pills too, as is one of my sisters.

Maybe I am sad not because I am congenitally unwell, but because I have seen so much. And felt it. Sometimes all this seeing fatigues me. But I never wish for a different experience. Instead, I just want a break. From reality, from clarity, from color. Or rather, I desire a medium to express what I've witnessed in a way that makes sense of the sadness. If I can render these visions using the right color palette, maybe my bruises can turn from vulgar red-purple to soft peach. I can't control the evils of the world, but I can try to be true to my story.

o

There is a color called Baker-Miller pink—younger sister to Pepto Bismol, a garishly girly bubblegum hue—named after two US Naval officers who, in 1979, studied the effects of pink walls on inmates. The two men ordered that a holding cell used for initial confinement of new inmates be painted completely pink, except for the floor. The cell housed new inmates for less than 15 minutes as they moved through processing. On day 156 of the experiment, the two wrote a memo indicating that no incidents of erratic or hostile behavior had occurred while detainees were held in the pink room. "The effect continues for fully thirty minutes after release from the cell!" the memo continued. "This is enough time to process the new inmate to a permanent cell." The study lasted for over two hundred days, and its findings continued to show that pink had magical powers.

In another study, this one performed at a university in 1991, exposure to pink (versus magnolia, a creamy, beige white) appeared to weaken muscle strength and promote docility. Many carceral institutions, as a result of this, have painted a cell pink, usually to hold inmates who have broken the rules of the institution. In Switzerland, I learn, one in five prisons and police stations have at least one pink cell.

Everything in prisons is controlled and is intended to control, even the colors inmates see.

o

In 2005, while flipping through a family photo album, the artist Alyse Emdur discovered the Polaroid that would define her art practice for the next eight years.

Scuffed and discolored, the once-white border frames a familiar tableau of the family photograph: the biggest kid—in this case, Emdur's much older brother—smiles in the middle, crouched low, with one arm around each of his two smaller siblings, the artist and her sister. Behind the trio, there's an orange sherbet sunset and the rippling blue ocean. A pair of black palms lean into the frame from above. It's the picture of a perfect family vacation. But the three aren't dressed for the beach. He wears jeans and a red polo shirt with white sneakers. His right knee rests not on sand, but on dark industrial flooring. The girls wear gray and white dresses, their white socks and tights tucked into shiny Sunday shoes.

The photograph was taken at Bayside State Prison in Leesburg, NJ where Emdur's brother was incarcerated. Over the next several years, the artist would correspond with hundreds of artists and visit twelve state prisons, where she used a large format camera to document the photo studios where inmates and their families captured their fleeting moments of togetherness. *Prison Landscapes*, the resulting artist's book, "offers viewers a rare opportunity to see America's incarcerated population, not through the usual lens of criminality, but through the eyes of inmates' loved ones."

Photos of inmates comprise "one of the largest practices of vernacular photography in the contemporary era," Fleetwood says. Yet the photographers—inmates themselves—are not recognized as artistic practitioners by the larger society, nor are those who paint the murals that serve as backdrops. Emdur probes these modes of painting and portraiture and illuminates this vast collection of works typically seen only by inmates, visitors, and employees. "Created specifically for escape and self-representation," Emdur writes, "the idealized paintings of tropical beaches, fantastical waterfalls, mountain vistas, and cityscapes invite sitters to perform fantasies of freedom." Awash in color, accompanied by family, the world of the visitor's room photograph is one where the light wins.

o

I had woken up early and consulted the inmate visitation guidelines to help me choose my outfit. No underwire bras. No blue. No showing midriff, cleavage, or thigh. No open-toe shoes. The list of no dragged on and made me anxious. I selected leopard print pants and a black long-sleeve thing that I wore to my job in an office at a nonprofit that was fanatic about its business casual dress code. Into a tote bag, I shoved a backup outfit.

In the parking lot, the regulars greeted each other. We huddled under umbrellas in the Oregon drizzle. We stood on the sidewalk and waited for the announcement over the loudspeaker that it was time to approach the building. We passed through one set of steel doors, then another. We put our car keys, coats, and umbrellas into the coin-op lockers. My dad handed me a plastic ziplock baggie full of quarters, so that I could buy coffee and gas station snacks from vending machines inside. The lockers were brown, the floor was brown, and everything else was gray.

A photographer is available to take photos that may be purchased at a later date, the visitor's guide said. I had prepared for my picture.

Our backdrop was a winter scene in which a low, wooden fence snakes around a cobalt pond and through a snow-white pasture bordered by young pine and fir, also white. On the back of the photo, he has written in pencil, "May 15th, 2011 I love you!! :)" The floor was the color of Werner's Yellowish White (see: egret, hawthorn blossom). His cheeks were pink. I was smiling. He was not. He wore Flax-Flower Blue.

o

In an essay by Lia Purpura entitled "On Looking Away: A Panoramic," I first encountered the Catholic concept of *custodia oculorum* or "custody of the eyes." Basically, it means choosing—and thus controlling—what you see. In religious terms, it's used devotionally in focused mediation on a sermon, or as a deterrent to sin, as in looking away from temptation. Do I have custody of my eyes? I struggle to look away from things that hurt me.

Purpura's essay is full of light and color, especially purples and greens. It elucidates a great many things she's seen that were difficult to look at, scenes of suffering, violence, and death. The piece ends with the author at eight years old enduring a punishment for expressing her feelings with too much vigor. Her mouth is washed out with soap, and she stares at a green spot on the sink while its suds are rinsed from her offending, pink tongue. "Even then I focused hard," she writes. "I felt I might be tested on what I saw."

o

One day, when I was feeling better, I went into Manhattan to see a show I'd been curious about. A couple of collaged pieces caught my eye in the exhibition preview—a surrealist scene of chartreuse snakes on a cherry red background and a daffodil yellow textile work overrun with amorphous blobs in a variety of patterns. They were cool enough in real life, but around a corner in the rear room of the gallery, a ceiling-high stanza of text rendered in white neon dwarfed the other work in the show and captured my attention in a way the collages hadn't. The plain white wall behind the text looked like dirty dishwater against the pristine glow of the lettering.

A thin strip of sky blue floated below the last line of the text suggesting a horizon, each word a flash of lightning. The sans serif text, though constructed so plainly in pristine white, was rife with violation. In the first two lines, a speaker is strip-searched by a corrections officer. Later lines contain screaming, fucking, punching, and sweating, but the meaning is ambiguous, its phrasing fragmentary. I was drawn to it because it was about both prison and bodily autonomy, a pure white display pregnant with the suggestion of blood-red institutional violence.

The work was by Sable Elyse Smith, an artist whose father was imprisoned for nineteen of her childhood and young adult years. I had encountered her work years earlier in *Marking Time*. Much of Smith's work focuses on the prison visiting room and other more subtly brutal, bureaucratic facets of the system. Like Emdur, she has created works from inmate photographs, but she also uses the materials of the space, particularly the tables, to create large-scale sculptures. "My interest is for people to look closer at these things and question them, and not just accept them as a necessity or an absolute," Smith says of the work. She wants custody of our eyes.

Of her table sculptures, Smith notes that their "design seems normal and neutral: a tabletop with stools connected to it. But the dimensions are skewed for visibility purposes. The tabletop comes very close to your knees, so it's harder for people to pass things under the table. Surveillance is baked into the design." Her 2021 kinetic sculpture, *A Clockwork*, gathers several such tables, painted a deep, inky black, in a shape that resembles a Ferris wheel, "a reference to the perpetuation of a loop, doing time, and the reliance on incarceration to produce capital." In a similar piece, the tabletops are painted blue. The blues resonate throughout Smith's body of work, showing up literally—as in the tables, her father's uniform in their family photos, and the streak of blue neon under white words—and also figuratively, as a lament for all that gets lost inside.

o

I stayed sad. Not sad, exactly, but clinically depressed. Worried about my well-being, my friend flew me out to visit her in Los Angeles. She rented us a cabin in Big Bear. She let me weep and complain. One day, we drove to a nature preserve, which turned out to be just a path between a lake and a highway, to watch the birds land on the water. Hardly any appeared. The sky was mostly gray, the water a Wernarian Greenish Black, rippling white where the wind pushed against it. At the end of the trip, I sat at her kitchen table where she pierced my skin with a sharp, silver needle. Above my knee, an image emerged: a black angel falling through a flesh-colored sky.

o

Shortly after I saw Smith's work in the gallery, I heard that the work from *Marking Time* was on display at the Schomburg Center for Research in Black Culture in Harlem. I went immediately.

The first room was dedicated to portraiture. Across the threshold, I was greeted first by a huge quilt of leather purse fragments (leather goods being common products of inmate labor), cut into four panels and painted over with a base layer of Dutch Orange splattered with drips of sky blue and indigo. Onto these panels, the formerly incarcerated artist Russell Craig had painted a self-portrait, his current self on the lower right panel, scratched into the trunk of a tree whose black branches reached up and across the top two panels. "Using penal matter like administrative documents to make art and penal time to become an artist, Craig transformed the limitations of prison—lack of materials, spatial constraints, surveillance, and the punitive regulation of time—into a place of artistic self-making," the wall text read.

Around the corner, I saw an Olatushani piece, even more vibrant than what was shown in the book, and a collection of orange hoodies designed by girls detained in a children's jail in Florida, among other works, some familiar, some novel. But the most striking of all these were the three or four walls covered from knee height to ceiling with basic hand-drawn portraits on standard 8.5x11 printer paper, the sort you'd buy on sale at Staples or steal from your office job. Across the room, I'd given the pieces a cursory glance and figured I'd need very little time to study them. They were simple, realistic, repetitive, and cameo-like. They framed their subjects from the bust up, in profile or at a quarter turn, and evoked the ballpoint and graphite prison drawings I'd seen a million times before.

But as I moved closer to these portraits, I became transfixed, not necessarily by their number, but by their mood. With his rounded pencil strokes and gently graduated shading, the artist had transformed the harsh institutional lighting into a glow that imbued the men with a seraphic softness. In opposition to the harshness of most mugshots, these images exuded a tenderness so tender that it brought a lump to my throat. Each face was undeniably unique, indicative of the artist's careful consideration. Each eyebrow and muscle suggested an individuated experience, despite the fact that each person had posed in the same general place and wore an identical shirt. I was surprised to see that very few faces showed anger, fear, or defensiveness. Instead, the faces looked relaxed, proud, hopeful, pensive, and, if sad, certainly not tortured.

Entitled *Pyrrhic Defeat: A Visual Study of Mass Incarceration*, the 725 drawings in this series (not all of which were on display) were done by Mark Loughney. The title references a theory by the same name, which analyzes how the rich and powerful benefit from the concept of criminalization. On the wall, I read that "Currently and formerly incarcerated artists have reinvigorated portraiture as a representational strategy to reflect on the massive toll that incarceration takes on the most marginalized groups while rendering them invisible in public life." Loughney added, "The irony is that 500 faces is not even a drop in the bucket of our 2.4 million brothers, mothers, sisters, and fathers that are locked away in prisons in our country."

Nearly all of the drawings were done in grayscale with pencil on white, with maybe five in blue or red ink and a few on ivory or limestone paper. It surprised me that such colorless work could capture me so totally, could take custody of not just my eyes, but my body.

The upper rooms of the exhibition housed two pieces by Smith, the blue table sculpture I recognized from *Marking Time*, and another white neon text piece underscored by a royal blue line, this one less a lament and more a song redolent with radiant futurity: "Someone smashed the policeman's radio / And finally silence A black language infinitely / And blue in a decade where it finally means sky."

There were dozens of pieces that deserved my attention. I spent time with all of them: Aimee Wissman's pen and ink postcards on pink paper—full of rage at her delayed release, their iconography inspired by Indigenous artists; Tameka Cole's collages punctuated with pops of red and orange; Ojore Lutalo's collaged posters, all of them created from solitary confinement. Looking back through the photos

I took, one stands out as particularly disturbing: a mixed media piece by Gilberto Rivera called *An Institutional Nightmare.* Assembled from prison uniforms, various papers, floor wax, and acrylic paint on canvas, the piece is lumpy, undulating, and chaotic. Its sandy brown, latex-glove yellow, poppy red, and ultramarine blue elements clash. It's hideous and disquieting. I think that's the point.

I have always adored ugliness. It is more interesting and true. Crooked teeth, a home-cut mohawk, patch-riddled clothes, malapropisms, paintings with impossible proportions, books about garbage or insanity or death. At the margins of beauty, the territory of the aberrant calls to me like wild dogs. Its baying is milky yellow in the moonlight, a blues song that carries me away into a dream.

o

It was in the second spring of my dark period that I decided, after much goading, to put together an art show. I had been crying for a year. Despite that, I had made fifteen tiles, each with one or two angels on it, with the exception of a single large square one that held seven small, impish spirits. While making these figures, I remembered the cheap porcelain and ceramic figurines in my grandmothers' houses, many of which were angels or other mass-produced home decors with prayerful connotations. A few were name-brand pieces, like Precious Moments or Hallmark, but most were of unknown manufacture, picked up at dollar stores or garage sales. My angels echoed the ivory and pastel colorways of these figurines. While I cut shapes with my tiny scissors and affixed them to sheets of gummy adhesive, I also thought about dozens of people I knew who had endured mental illness, substance abuse disorders, and other difficulties before me. I drew upon their power during my depression.

However, my angels differed significantly from the Christian symbols from which they derived. Growing up in the church, I admired many of the spiritual principles espoused by the scripture and took comfort in the idea of benevolent divinity, but I was bothered by the more oppressive parts of the teachings. My angels—with their mixed-up genitals and contorted wings—were genderless, agnostic alternatives to those of my childhood. They were the guardian angels I had always wanted.

Using money from an artist's grant that was otherwise paying most of my rent, I rented a small space in Brooklyn for a single Monday night in May. I asked friends and friends-of-friends to show their work. We each took on a production task, and in our hands, the show came off perfectly. People were invited, and they came. Dozens, maybe even a couple hundred. The other artists' work was strange and reverent, much of it colorful. Together, our work represented a full range of hue.

In the weeks before the show, I had put together a zine of my pieces and had it printed on nice paper. I sold them on a table under the big windows opposite my angels. I felt more proud of this work than anything I'd ever done, and it felt truer than any words I'd ever been able to string together—before or since. The tile glowed under a strip of tube lights covered over with pink film, the wings of the angels cutting slashes of black, blue, brown and blush into the field of white. I had never seen them on a wall. Suspended like that, they really looked like they were flying.

In the weeks following the show, I noticed something. I wasn't crying anymore.

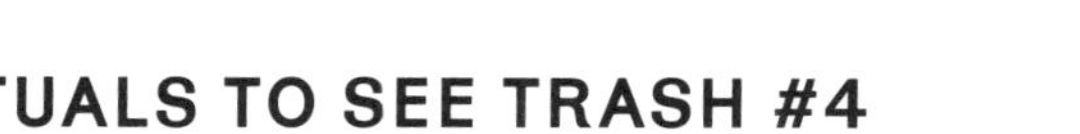
RITUALS TO SEE TRASH #4

1. For a sentence of six months, commit to wearing monochromatic clothing in penal hues, limiting yourself to one color per month. Color options include cornflower blue, Dutch orange, Baker-Miller pink, gunmetal gray, primary red, padded-room white, and institutional beige.

Optional Extension: paint the walls of your bedroom to match your clothing each month.

2. Document your outfit every morning. Throughout the day, take notes about how the color of your clothes is affecting your life. You might note your mood, your imagination, your sex drive, your work performance, or the way others treat you. Do not let this list be exhaustive.

4. After your sentence is over, continue to take notes for two weeks as you readjust to a lifestyle in which all color is permitted.

5. If you remain haunted by this experiment, throw your clothing and documentation in the trash. Notice whether this aids your recovery—if you are able to forget.

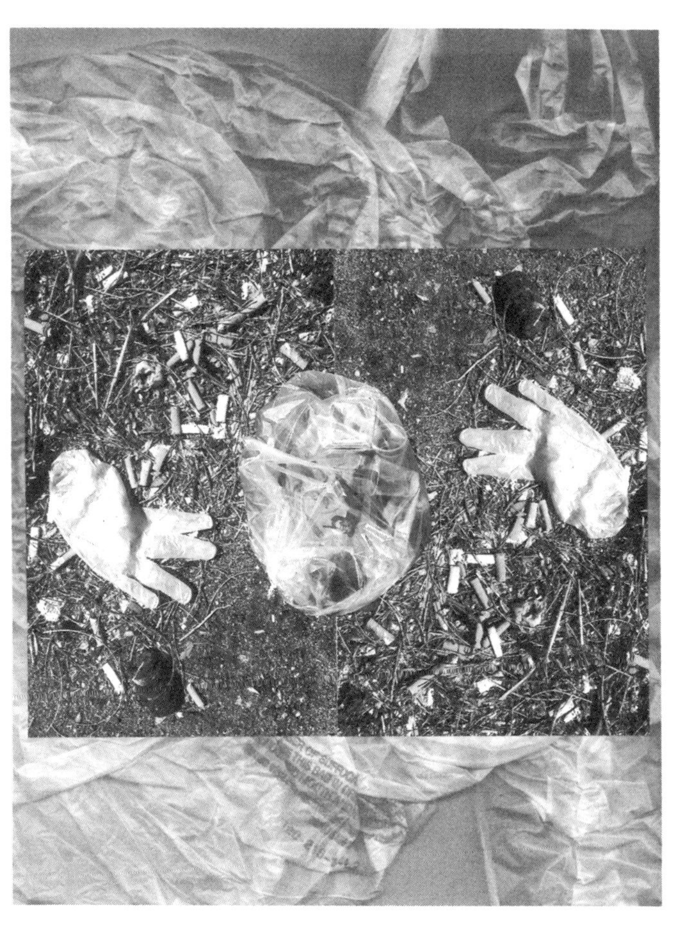

ON HOLES

○ Holes as Opportunity ○

They were called "gutter pieces." For the first one, Pope L. sat in half-lotus on a filthy sidewalk in front of a commercial gallery in New York City's Soho neighborhood. He wore a business suit. Inside a ring of wooden matches, the artist rested on a small square of yellow cloth. He laid out his shoes, a paper bag, bottles of Thunderbird and Wild Irish Rose, a can of Coca-Cola, and a measuring cup. For the duration of *Thunderbird Immolation a.k.a. Meditation Square Piece*, the performance captured in the first photograph I ever saw of him, Pope L. periodically meditated, doused himself with alcohol, and spelled out words with the matches.

The unwanted, unhoused, insane, or injured occupy the ground in public—those with other options prefer to rest in higher places. It was from this unclean place, at the gutters of art and commerce, at the border between insider and out, that Pope L. made lack a performance, a protest, and a prayer. The low-budget booze he used to mime self-immolation is a hallmark of corner stores in poor neighborhoods, a symbol of how capital conspires to rob the working class of their very lives. As he claimed ground for art and grabbed death by the balls, Pope L. paid homage to people who wrest dignity from a closed fist, even while they live in utter abjection. *You can't kill me, motherfucker,* the piece seems to say. *Only I can do that.*

And yet, there are lower places to go than the gutter. You can go underground. You can go to the hole.

Pope L. went there on a hot August day in 1996, when he donned a dress shirt and tie, then dug a hole deep enough to stand in. He got into the hole and was buried up to his shoulders, his arms pinned to his sides under the dirt. A dish of vanilla ice cream was then placed a few inches in front of his face. For the next few hours, all he could do was watch while it slowly melted in the sun, his body compressed underground, his head baking under its red cap. Pope L. opens the video documenting this performance, entitled *Sweet Desire a.k.a. Burial Piece*, with questions about desire and lack: "What do black people want?" "Who do they want it from?" "Why do they want it?" This performance is his response to these questions. Or perhaps it is not an answer, but an escalation. An expansion.

"I do not picture the hole. I am the hole," he wrote in his 2002 art book *Hole Theory*, a small artifact that includes drawings, scribbles, dialogues, and definitions. Composed in a circulatory, poetic style and line-edited by hand, *Hole Theory* feels eternally in process. Rather than thinking of holes as wounds or misfortunes, Pope L sees them as conduits, intersections, occasions, and jesterly tricks, each iteration a whole new arena for the imagination. His work suggests that holes are good, and he imbues them with good ideas, good energy, and good action.

Above all else, Pope L. was interested in the lack epitomized by holes and in the potential of that empty space. "I am interested in holes because I have been wounded by absence," he writes. "Marked by this trauma, I have a choice: either be ruled by circumstance or be circumstance and tap the energy of predicament, make it my pet, my posey, my theory—no remorsey." Holes are pure potential, then, even though they are born of nothingness. He jumps right in.

I am also interested in holes, but unlike Pope L., their misuse animates me more than the opportunities they present. Holes are only fun when they are filled with the right things.

◦ Holes as Places of Rest ◦

I once had a boyfriend named James whose father Ed died indigent somewhere near San Francisco. That was the thing about Ed—some of the details were always fuzzy. He kept a small, black handgun in the freezer, for example, when James was a child, but the houses where the guns were stored remained mysterious. He inhabited each only vaguely—as a squatter or temporary visitor, never as a lease-holder or owner. These dwellings could probably have been called shitholes. Their addresses were quickly forgotten. Ed was a lifelong drug user who frequented jails and seemed to feel belonging amid the alterity of the streets. He didn't believe in jobs, taxes, or apartments. He preferred vagrancy, as much as one can prefer it to being born or sliding into it and, again, the details of Ed's route to the bottom were not all there.

Ed listed James as his next of kin while he lay dying in state-funded hospice. Ed had been cremated at the county's expense, and James needed to be present to sign some paperwork and claim the plastic bag that held what was left of his dad, now a coarse mix of gray ashes. Unable to fly on such short notice, James attempted to transfer kinship to a relative who lived locally. They failed to meet the deadline.

A year or two later, I asked James if he knew what happened to Ed's unclaimed ashes. Did he end up in a hole in a communal cemetery? Was he tossed into the Bay or locked away in a vault? "They dumped him somewhere. That's what they said they would do." He trailed off. He wandered into the bathroom and got something out of the cabinet. "They were rude and unhelpful," he said, "so I don't know." He said that he didn't want to talk anymore about it.

I didn't bring it up again, but Ed's missing ashes got me thinking about holes and what kinds of things we are inclined to put into them. It got me thinking about how hard it can be to find something again once it's gone to ground and wondering if, as Pope L. suggests, the hole can be reclaimed as a generative space, even while its obliterative power seems to reign supreme. If holes are a fact of life and death, what could be made of them? Where could the art come in?

∘ Holes as Human Beings ∘

The cover of the Summer 2022 issue of *Artforum* shows a white carnation floating on diminutive dark blue waves. The flower had been thrown into the Long Island Sound by the artist Coco Fusco, who rowed a boat out onto the water to perform a Catholic funeral rite for the million-odd people interred on Hart Island—New York's potter's field—as well as for her friend who had recently died. A drone camera captured footage of her from above while she tossed carnations onto the waves, the sun shining on her curly black hair, the boat a feather on the water, the grass of the island a stirring, springy green.

The term *potter's field* is Biblical. It refers to an actual, specific field called Akeldama which means *field of blood* in Aramaic. The Bible's Book of Matthew tells us that while the condemned Jesus was being taken to Pilate, Judas repented. He took the silver coins he'd been paid for turning over Jesus to the priests as part of his penance. Reluctant to put the money into the temple coffer "because it is the price of blood," the priests used it to buy a "potter's field" for use as a burying place for "strangers" (read: non-Jews, criminals, and the poor) who died in Jerusalem. The field they chose, Akeldama, had been a source of potter's clay. Once the clay was removed, it was a wasteland, unusable for agriculture or construction. The ground was full of trenches and holes, and so it was a ready-made graveyard for god's un-chosen ones: those who, because of reputation, religion, or class, would not receive an orthodox burial.

Like me, Fusco became interested in Hart Island and its holes during the early days of the pandemic that began in 2020, when she saw images of inmates—presumably the same ones I saw on the news, the captives of Rikers in white hazmat suits, black dirt falling from the shining spades of their shovels—burying people who had recently died. Inside the simple pine boxes buried on the island were immigrants, other inmates, the unhoused, and similarly hard-up, low-life people. "It has been a dumping ground for every class of human being that the larger society has wanted to reject," Fusco said of the island. "People who were diseased, people who were considered criminal, people who were unwanted have [all] been housed there in one way or another." The mass graves at Hart Island had not been open since the height of the AIDS crisis, but there they were, open again.

Your Eyes Will Be An Empty Word, the video essay she created from the performance, uses drone footage of the island and Fusco's funerary ceremony to explore the relationship between holes, power, and forgetting. Rather than staging the piece on Hart Island, Fusco chose to throw flowers from a boat in part because the island is so difficult to access. There are some holes that the ruling class would rather we didn't peer into, full of things they would like us to forget.

◦ Holes as Words ◦

Life at the margins is rife with hole language. Prisoners who misbehave are sent to the hole. One can be in the hole, meaning in debt. An ill-funded business is a hole-in-the-wall. A hole is a fix, a scrape, or a mess. A hole is a lowly hovel where hole people live with holes in their socks and cavities in their teeth and bullet holes in their backs.

◦ Holes as Home ◦

Pope L.'s most notable early work was *Times Square Crawl a.k.a. Meditation Square Piece*, which he staged to highlight the housing crisis in late 1970's New York.

He recalls the era as one of extreme dereliction. Buildings crumbled and caught fire. Garbage filled the gutters. People slept in rows so dense on the city's sidewalks that one had to literally step over them.

For the performance, the artist crawled on his hands and knees along 42nd Street, the Square's most famous thoroughfare, again wearing business attire with the same yellow fabric from *Thunderbird Immolation* pinned to his back. Documentation shows confused onlookers—their faces alive with concern and disgust—as well as police who intervened to see what the hell was going on. I can't judge them for responding with bewilderment. Why would any sane, respectable person, in this case a Black businessman, inhabit the ground, especially the smog-thick, clamorous, sticky understory of a struggling, pre-gentrified New York?

Their confusion was compounded by what Pope L. calls "verticality"—the wealth and privilege that keeps some of us upright and mobile, insulated from the horizontal crawl-and-stall existence of the hole classes. He staged the work because he'd noticed that "We'd gotten used to people begging, and I was wondering, how can I renew this conflict? I don't want to get used to seeing this. I wanted people to have this reminder." By occupying the hole space, he hoped to trip people up, challenging them to re-envision the man-made tragedy of modern suffering that they had tacitly accepted as fact. Pope L. crawled into the hole and animated it, turning a worn, mute orifice into a screaming mouth.

The performance was short (Pope L. crawled only until he was stopped by a cop), but brevity amplified its depth. Observers were quick to intervene on a man in a suit disinheriting his vertical privilege. "The abject position in which the artist placed himself—slinking along the floor amidst the litter, grime, and sewage systems of the metropolis—highlighted the plight of people living on the streets, of which members of the artist's own family had occasionally been subject," wrote art critic Jessica Holmes, reflecting on the performance. His brother, aunt, and father all lived on the streets during this period. Pope L. feared running into them and didn't know what he'd do or say if he did. I can relate. I wonder if the crawl was a deliberate search for his loved ones and an effort to regain control of the situation by encountering them down there, on their turf, among the refuse and grit, the vulnerable act held safely inside the container of his creative practice. For Pope L., then, holes are personal. They are home.

◦ Holes as Hideaways ◦

Ever since I started writing about art and trash, I have wanted to go to a landfill. One can win a residency at certain waste management centers, but I wanted the raw, unfiltered experience. Just before a trip I took to see family in Las Vegas, I learned that the largest landfill in the United States, and one of the largest in the world, is located northeast of the city. Apex (note: not nadir) Regional Landfill can accept 15 thousand tons of waste per day and is supposed to last two hundred years. That's a big hole and a lot of trash, slowly morphing from hollow to mountain. I was hole-curious. So, I asked for a tour.

Of course, they said no. They said, "Thank you for reaching out! Unfortunately, we are not able to assist with your request. However, we do have videos online and other resources on our website that may be helpful to you. Have a great day!" I was annoyed, but not surprised. Like Hart Island and most carceral institutions, landfills are not accessible to the general public. I imagine they don't want people seeing how much garbage there really is. They don't want people to smell it or ask questions about it, and they don't want people to see the sanitation workers toiling on its dusty rim.

Since I couldn't go to the landfill, I opted to study it using satellite imaging. This, too, was a slippery proposition. Its remote location and proximity to other industrial enterprises complicated my search. I couldn't discern where the landfill began or ended. It took diligence, but I finally found the open cell at Apex that was accepting fresh trash. What I saw was unremarkable—a patch of lilac-blue roughness amid miles and miles of red-brown desert soil. I sat there for a while, leaning in close to the screen, zeroed in on the open cell. Then I sat back and zoomed way out. I wanted to see how many clicks it took for Apex to disappear into the desert. It didn't take very many at all, maybe two or three. Unless you are looking very carefully, one of the largest holes in the world is almost impossible to see.

○ Holes as Resistance ○

In "The Image and the Void," Vietnamese filmmaker and writer Trinh T. Minh-ha digs around inside work that is "multiplicity in resistance—via the seen, the barely seen, and the unseen; in the between, the margins, and the borders of visible reality; and through the power of blanks, holes, silences, and empty spaces." Like Pope L., Minh-ha leaps into the negative, finding that the hole is a cypher in the mathematical sense, the zero that is of no value by itself, but which increases or decreases the value of what's around it based on its position. "Worth noting is the recurrence on the world stage of such features as the lone chair and the unoccupied seat; the blank page, blank space, bland sign; the screen gone white, with no content; the empty frame or the frame with no art; and last but not least, the interval of silence—all potentially endowed with a powerfully haunting effect." The goal, then, of the oppressor, is to close the hole as soon as possible, to staunch the haunt before it can reveal the depth of our deprivation (or excess or complicity) and drive us all stark-raving mad. I like to think of the artist as an antidote to this poisoned forgetting, helping us recall and commemorate all that's been buried alive.

∘ Holes as Vessels ∘

Ugly jugs, also known as memory vessels, forget-me-not jugs, or spirit jars, are funerary objects of folk art once common in the American South. The jugs I have seen are, in fact, ugly. To make one, a vessel is first covered with a layer of adhesive—something like cement, putty, plaster, or clay. Onto this muddy substrate, the maker presses pieces of the decedent's possessions: buttons, brushes, coins, pendants, tools, lockets, and other small, sometimes broken, ephemera. The result is pell-mell and lumpy, often very brown, and composed of coarse, quotidian materials. Still, their ugliness shines.

"It's easy to conclude that memory jugs existed as inexpensive memorials for poor families who couldn't afford headstones for loved ones," writes one historian, but there is more to the story. They were accessible, affordable objects, but they were also meaningful emblems of the cultural practices of enslaved people with Bakongo roots in Central and West Africa. The Bakongo used similar vessels as grave markers. One belief undergirding these totems was that the spirit world was upside down and connected to this one by water. Hollow vessels were thus left at graves to help the dead tread their watery way into the afterlife. Items the deceased might find useful in the next realm were placed along with the vessels, all of it upside down, with pieces broken to symbolically release the spirit.

These traditional funerary rites melded with the "Southern custom of using ceramic grave markers as inexpensive alternatives to stone slab headstones" and popular Victorian craft to produce the ugly jug. In the US, "The fragmented possessions, reconformed in the memory jug, paid homage to and simultaneously appeased the spiritual beings, encouraging them not to interfere with the lives of the living." Absent honor, holes are alive with vengeful ghosts. It's only a matter of time before they strike.

Ed used to live in a tent at the dump. I know little about this, except that he managed to have a working television inside. As with the topic of his cremains and where they might be, it was hard to get James to talk about this.

We never found out what happened to Ed's ashes. What my ex and I had is long gone. Writing about him is part of how I heal, which is a type of forgetting and also a type of remembrance. My art is a hole. I can put mementos inside and affix them to its edges. I can make an ugly jug to memorialize my lack.

∘ Holes as Beds to Dream In ∘

Once, when my therapist asked me how I was feeling, I said that I wanted to lie in a hole and have someone chuck dirt on top of me. "Sounds like a grief ritual," she said. "What are you grieving?" A list of options spun through my head, and I did not know which one to say.

While I wrote this essay, Pope L. passed away at age 68, nine years shy of the current 77-year life expectancy for people in the States. He was born working-class in 1955 in Newark, New Jersey to an absentee dad and a mom with a taste for oblivion. "My family life was very uncertain," he said in an interview from 1996. "I'll never get rid of that uncertainty. We never knew from one moment to the next when we would move, what we were going to eat… You grow up scared. You realize that there's not much difference between you and street people." Pope L's difficult early upbringing moved him to create the work that he did, but the lack he experienced may have also foreshortened the time he had to work.

Those with wealth and other privileges enjoy their verticality. They live several years longer, on average, than those with a more lowly "political condition." The number of years that money can buy is somewhere between eight and 15. What would you do with your extra time?

I would lie in the grass and stare at the sky and think about how high it really goes. I would write another book and it wouldn't be about trash and suffering and dying; it would be about butterflies. I would build a vessel out of trash and sail across the sea. I would learn more about art and Pope L. and dig more holes and plant a memorial garden in his name.

Pope L. continued to make work about holes and crawl on the ground long after the 1970s. He earned tremendous success: a retrospective at MoMa, two appearances at the Whitney Biennial, notable work in several media, a handful of controversies, and grants for tens of thousands of dollars. He made holey work that confounded, disturbed, and poked fun at us so that we could more clearly see the predicament of our relationships to one another, particularly along the fault lines of race and class.

"Entitlement's gift to the majoritarian subject is the psychic denial of the lack at the core of the self," writes the art critic Jennifer Doyle. "It is the ability to operate with the illusion of wholeness and transparency." The ethical position to take, then, as audience to art and life, is one that insists on "the gap, the negative, the nonalignment and opacity of the subject," to admit the hole and embrace it. To study it. To be it.

Holeness: the shapely voids left by shoplifters on mega-mart shelves. The ring-filled gouges in our badly set noses. The highway air coursing through our holes, gas tank verging on void. Maybe Pope L.

was correct, and "lack is where it's at." Wholeness is the illusory prerogative of the privileged class, with their mouths full of teeth and their houses full of art and their accounts full of cash. We inhabit that other place. Welcome to the hole.

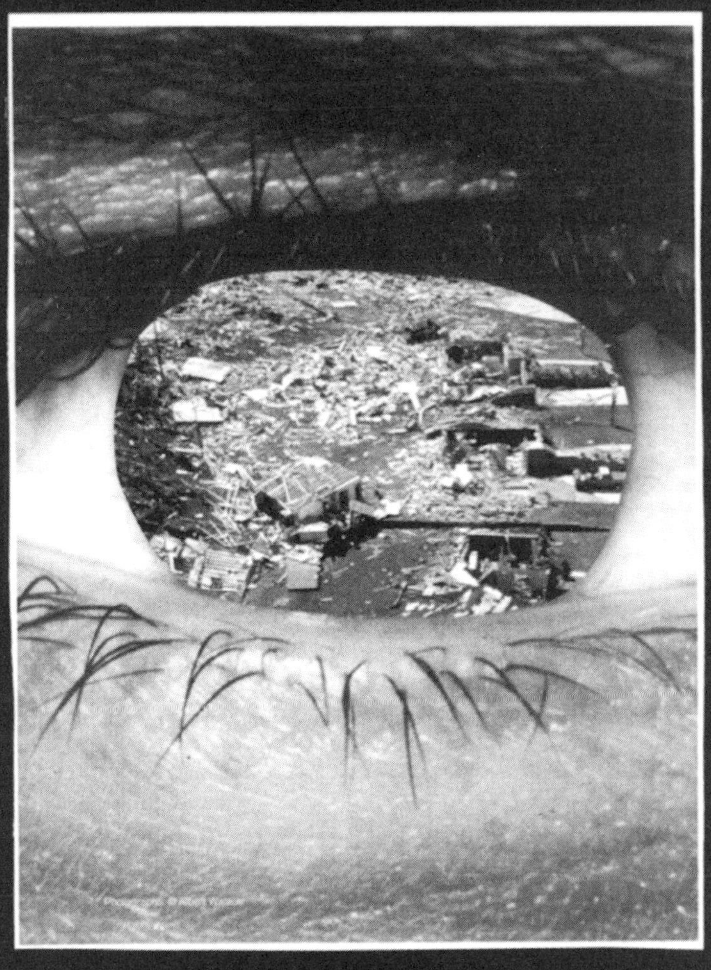

RITUALS TO SEE TRASH #5

1. For one week, instead of throwing it away or recycling it, keep all disposable plastic you use in your purse. If you do not carry a purse, a briefcase or backpack is acceptable. Pockets will likely not be sufficient.

2. As you run out of room in your bag, dump the plastic into your bathtub.

3. After one week, remove all your clothing and lie down in the tub. Remain still to let your body absorb the shape and texture of your refuse. Take photos of the imprints that the various plastics leave on your skin.

Optional Extension: have the imprints tattooed.

THE ART OF WAR

I am on my way home from work when two teenage girls get on the bus wearing orange safety vests with LABORER DSNY (Dept. of Sanitation New York) printed on them. I wonder if they are doing mandatory community service, picking up litter from the gutters, because nothing about the way they look, from their long, pink nails to their soft, fuzzy boots, says that this is voluntary, and would DSNY employees be taking the city bus? Glittery cell phone cases. Pony beads. Heavy breath. If there wasn't so much trash, if there were no laws, what would they be doing with their time? The girls cram together in the seat across the aisle. Behind them, out the window, we pass one long, gray building after another. Amazon distribution center. Federal Express. Unmarked cinder block monstrosity. Housing projects. Fenced-off land, stolen by massacre, then zoned commercial and left vacant. A few months after it closed, Fresh Kills Landfill on Staten Island, just across the water from me on this bus in Brooklyn, reopened to accept the debris from 9/11, an event which was used to launch a war that never ended, a war that wasted more than can ever be counted. Hundreds of thousands of lives. Millions of barrels of jet fuel. Decommissioned ships. Abandoned barracks. Ration remnants. Idle tanks rusting in the desert outside Twentynine Palms, Baghdad, and who knows how many other places. The conversation about garbage often focuses on consumer goods, not on the vast military and industrial waste created in service of profits. My grandfather, now deceased, enlisted to fight the war in Vietnam. He didn't die there, but he was exposed to chemicals and other horrors that killed him slowly, over many decades, like any of the other wasting diseases. What is a war, really? So much of the everyday business of modern life requires violence. None of us can opt out of participating—it's just how things work. It has been estimated that each American generates something like five pounds of garbage each day, every day that they are alive. I had a hard time visualizing this until I read that I will need one gravesite when I die, but my garbage will fill over a thousand. All those plots and their gravestones are easy for me to picture. I'd like to write "I'm Sorry" on all the headstones, but maybe "Not guilty" would fit better. If you could throw away less, wouldn't you? Waste Management, Inc. Dow Chemical. Exxon Mobil. Bayer. Nestlè. Tesla. Some companies waste more than others. On my phone, the press speculates that war is imminent. I read the headline and the lede, then continue down the infinite scroll of bellicose prophecy and related reports. Wheat rations. Energy insecurity. Nuclear options. I am encouraged to sign up for the Russia-Ukraine War Briefing. Inmate road work dates back to an 1887 law requiring courts to sentence less serious criminals to hard labor on the county roads and highways. At least that's what I find on a website maintained by the state of South Carolina. The Thirteenth Amendment. Jim Crow. Shoplifting can get you jailed or killed, as can selling CDs, driving, working at a fast food restaurant, sleeping, and having a disability, especially if you aren't white. What I mean is: I hate it here, a country that makes people do beautiful, desperate things, and only metes out more punishment. Bless these girls if they are earning an honest living doing something they love, but who in America is doing that today? In 2003, former US Secretary of State Colin Powell delivered a PowerPoint presentation to the United Nations Security Council, deploying fabricated evidence to prove the presence of weapons of mass destruction in Iraq and justify an American invasion. While he spoke, UN officials covered up a tapestry reproduction of Pablo Picasso's *Guernica*, one of the world's most renown anti-war paintings, that hangs outside the Council. *I pledge allegiance to the flag of the United States of America.* I see garbage everywhere: broken copy machine, broken computers, electronic waste on cargo ships bound for the great continent of Africa. Candy wrappers stuck in a cyclone fence. Empty storefronts with their windows papered over. The United States has nearly two thousand active landfills. I've pored over hundreds of charts, photographs, papers, and reports trying to understand them. One thing I now know, but can't truly fathom, is that our landfills leak poisonous fluid into the soil and water at a rate of up to 60 million liters per site per day. Endrin. Dieldrin. Clotrimazole. Tetrabromobisphenol-A. DDE. DDT. Tetracycline. The industrial byproducts of cigarette making. I read a study the other day that explained why it's difficult to determine the effects of living near a landfill on humans. It was about exposure, duration, and the element of chance. We don't know how each body will react to toxins, but study or not, everyone knows, deep down, that this is fatal. How many chemicals are you exposed to each day, and how do you cope? A man coughs and vomits on the subway floor. He dry heaves for over fifteen minutes. Yellow bile. Invisible particles. Viral loads. I think about calling for help, but I am scared of what might happen at the hands of the police, the hospitals. Out the window, I see the contents of an entire apartment on the curb. I wonder briefly if the tenants were evicted. It's relentless. I've never been on Randall Island, over there, where they used to send all the homeless and people with disabilities back in the day of state-run poorhouses. Out of sight, out of mind. A cargo ship carrying 1,100 Porsches and other luxury cars is burning adrift in the Atlantic. Grand church. Grand Army Plaza. Tunnel carved from stone. Grand Central. Wind-worn trash dangling from the trunks of the trees at the edges of the ravines like seaweed or party streamers. Happy late capitalism. Happy death day. Happy birthday balloons are one of many cheap, disposable items made using American prison labor. Waste Not, Want Not. Toll bridge overhead. Concrete risers. A dozen identical delivery vans parked under an overpass. The Highbridge Train Wash Facility where they powerwash the graffiti off the cars with chemicalized water. Which chemicals? A chlorine plant in New Jersey caught fire and is still burning. No evacuation, no casualties: at least that's the official message. There are vast military burn pits outside Mosul, Tikrit, Mogadishu, Djibouti, Abu Ghraib. Every American military outpost. Scorched surplus. Burning tires. Cardboard. Plastic tarps. Metal cylinders, grayed with ash. Melted plastic water bottles, thousands of them. Veterans with severe neurological symptoms. Black smoke in the pink lungs of a baby. Stone arches reinforced with steel girders.

Brick towers. Construction and demolition accounts for a significant portion of waste globally, but I can't find an exact number. It's cheaper, by some metrics, for some people, to throw things away rather than reuse them. Warning: US Coast Guard Restricted Area. What makes people pick comfort over integrity, money over eternity? I don't understand it. I think World War III started yesterday, or maybe it's been happening this whole time. It's merely my perception or awareness that changes. A reporter interviewed dozens of people at Ukraine's border with Poland, mostly younger men, who were willingly returning from abroad to take up arms against the Russians. Molotov cocktails. Machine guns. A bomb goes off at an apartment complex, and in the red smoke, I see shards of ruin fluttering like butterflies in a storm. What would you die for, and why that? Acres of naked winter trees. A wastewater treatment plant. American Sugar Refining, Inc. Alryan Lubricants. Some other industrial outfit with no signage. *And to the Republic for which it stands.* Where are all the guns made? Who makes the tanks, the helicopters, the drones? Ice on the river rocks. Ice cubes made with charcoal-filtered water—the stuff that comes out of the tap in my apartment smells faintly of swimming pool. Rough water. Small craft advisory. If I fell into the river, how long til I'd die? The Iraqi artist Dia al-Azzawi was not in his home country on the day of Powell's pro-war presentation in 2003. He had fled to England in the late 1970s because he intuited that Iraq would soon slip into totalitarianism, a political environment that would create, among other problems, a world in which art served only to glorify heads of state. He was correct, unfortunately. There was a war with Iran, international sanctions, then Powell, the Americans, and their murderous drones. Sometimes I have the most absurd thoughts. Sometimes they are interrupted by the train conductor. Next stop Croton-Harmon. How things are named and who after: everything has a story. Using an online tool created by the EPA, I find the names of 45 active Superfund sites at waste management facilities where human exposure is not yet under control: Argonaut Mine, Armstrong World Industries, Beck's Lake, Big River Mine Tailings, Estech General Chemical Company. Pine trees out the window, suddenly—why? I have always been interested in microclimates, science talk. "Amoeba" by the Adolescents is one of my favorite punk songs. Even in small towns like Cortlandt, someone outfitted all the benches with anti-homeless arm rests. People do things like this. Banal cruelties. Engineered suffering. Can you explain it? Beggars can't be choosers. It destroys me, psychologically. The first landfill ever to open in the US is now a Superfund site. It's in Fresno, California. Gravel parking lots. Old army forts. Vacation homes. Jeep Grand Cherokee. The Grand Old Flag, high-flying. Cell phone towers. The sky is a brilliant cornflower color. According to the *Times*, the United States and its allies have, in recent days, discussed a litany of sanctions they will impose if Russia invades Ukraine. These include cutting off large Russian banks from global transactions, "imposing an embargo on American-made or American-designed technology needed for defense-related and consumer industries," and arming Ukrainian insurgents to wage guerrilla warfare against the Russian military "if it comes to that." The train stutters and stalls. The speaker over which the conductor talks is broken, and it emits high-pitched static. Orange plastic in the water. A factory across. I have a lot of respect for big states with hardly anything in them. Wyoming. Oregon. North Dakota. Many larger states with low population density become repositories for the garbage produced by and for major metropolitan areas, including nuclear waste. Some of New York's trash goes to Ohio and Virginia. Former mining sites. Convenient holes. Before he left Iraq, Azzawi had lived in Mosul for two years, where he helped start a new archaeological museum and generally involved himself in the ancient city's art scene. Later, he watched these great halls of culture succumb to sectarian violence. Shattered statues. Looted artifacts. Burned books. I wish this was hard to imagine. Some trees reach up from the river water. It must have flooded. Trash bobs among the sticks and branches: yellow oil container, blue ball, white hull of a little boat. The river licks the toes of the train as it passes. I often feel that I'm on a movie set, and I wonder if that's a symptom of having done too many psychedelics. Did I feel like this when I was a young teenager, before I did the bulk of the damage? School bells were developed to condition working class children like me to respond to whistles at factories and to stick to arbitrary, rigid schedules. I watched with amazement when my high school students moved automatically from one room to another at the signal and although I was charged with keeping them in line, I sometimes cheered inside when they rebelled against such structures. I hope I never become inured to violence. White smoke, exhaled from a stack. A silver sculpture in a riverside park. The wind is moving south. I try to capture the light on the water, first with my iPhone, then with my heart. The name Garrison implies a store of weapons. Is that a lie? I am not that old, and yet I already feel my memory slipping. Alzheimer's terrifies me, but it doesn't run in my family. How will I go? Arthritis, heart valve weakness, COPD, brain aneurysm, detached retinas. Cancer from exposure to god knows how many chemicals. A dozen mansions on a hill crest. A freight train whistle. Old fashioned telephone poles made of now-rotting wood. We made all this, and we will destroy it. The Metro North train platforms have little glass shelters for frigid days like these. Blue ice, black ice, brown ice. Paper plates and napkins frozen inside a puddle. Newspapers/bottles/trash on a green trio of metal containers. White-covered boats in a storage facility. People protect what they value. A big piece of property with several outbuildings. Retired machinery. What are those machines called that have the big claw? Such technology is necessary to landfill operations. Rust Belt is kind of a cruel name, now that I think about it. We throw around the most hurtful language. Peekskill seems cruel, but actually the Dutch word *kill* means stream. I learned that researching landfills. Navy blue hills in the distance. White snowpack. How can I describe the color of this water? A stack of oily railroad ties. What is creosote? What is color? What is the point? Carson River Mercury Site, FE Warren Air Force Base,

Freeway Sanitary Landfill, Gary Development, Jacksonville Ash Site, Makah Reservation Warmhouse Beach Dump, Oronogo-Duenweg Mining Belt. *One nation, under god, indivisible.* There are over five hundred Superfund sites on tribal lands, not all of them landfills, and that doesn't even count the catastrophes that are intentionally kept secret. I need a way to exist that means something, a record of what I witnessed. Here it is. Orange traffic cone. Orange work vests. Gray trains. Gray sky. Powder blue corrugated steel. Gray seats. As an artist, I have very little discipline. I am so scared of myself, that everything has to come out in leaps and bursts, otherwise I strangle it. Between 2004 and 2007, Azzawi created a work called *Mission of Destruction* that depicts the demolition of Mosul. It looks like *Guernica*. Overlapping outlines of hundreds of contorted limbs occupy one side of the canvas, opposite a rigid group of abstracted, armed soldiers. The immense painting (measuring approximately 8 by 50 feet), protests US military occupation and laments the loss of seven thousand years of civilization. After two days upstate, I return to the city. At first, the chaos overwhelms me, but it doesn't take long to regain my footing. More housing projects. Uber headquarters. Harlem-125th Street. Stained glass. Copper statues of American heroes, some greater than others. The insanity of the wires. Overflowing trash cans. Plastic bags caught in the fingers of all the trees. A brick building named after a warmonger. Miles of underground tunnel networks. Electrified tracks. "Final stop. Take all your personal belongings with you when you go." A forty-year-old Asian woman died after being pushed in front of a subway on Saturday morning. Murdered. "Do you have any change, any snacks or candy?" he asks the woman across from me. He asks the air, the door. This is his prayer. What is mine? What is yours? I don't have anything on me today; good luck to you. Last year, when I had more money, I always kept change and bills in my pockets, for one because I believe in the redistribution of resources, even in tiny amounts, and for two, it keeps me from incurring the wrath of some people. It is worth much more than $.87, $1 to have a nice interaction with someone, especially someone who is so uncomfortable, so forsaken. Glossy, chapped lips. Hair thick with grease. Shoes without laces. My middle class guilt is dangerous. Am I even middle class? What does that mean? Climate anxiety is a middle-class issue. Garbage is not a worry, but a material reality for billions of people globally. Zaza Exotics. Dominoes. AutoZone. Kiwi Valley Deli & Grocery Corp. So many places to buy things in packages to throw away later. Royal Garbage Carting Service. Six thousand identical apartments. Is that a lie? Who knows how many. Less than 10% of landfills in the US are equipped to capture and process methane, a greenhouse gas ten times more potent than carbon dioxide, and a natural byproduct of trash as it rots underground. In nations where dumping is less regulated, explosions and fires are frequent. People who live on and around them die under the smoldering rubbish. I've watched survivors of dump explosions interviewed on the news. They sob, and their tears cut clean, clear ruts into their dusty faces while they gesture at the detritus. If your home exploded, where would you go? All landfills will eventually leak, poisoning soil and groundwater. I try to put myself in the shoes of someone who is growing wealthy as a direct result of all this waste. *With liberty and justice for all.* The Amazon. The Ganges. Kabul. Kandahar. Hiroshima. Gora Prai. Managua. Phnom Penh. Qeycad. Agent Orange sprayed on green Vietnamese jungle that ate my granddad's insides out. What kind of luxury could be enough to justify it? How many dollars? In Salish culture a burial is called a planting. Safety is a lie. We ingest at least 50 thousand microplastic particles every year, or something like a credit card worth of plastic each week. Petro-Processors of Louisiana, Sand Creek Industrial, Sauer Dump, South Dayton Dump and Landfill, Route 561 Dump, Sulphur Bank Mercury Mine, Utah Power and Light. Plastic doesn't ever biodegrade, but it does fracture into ever-smaller particles when exposed to wind, sun, and moisture. These microplastics contaminate drinking water, including the water that gets bottled inside more plastic. In the United States, 94 percent of tap water samples now contain plastic fibers. I don't know the statistics for Indonesia, Mongolia, Brazil, Costa Rica, Ghana. Shellfish eat ocean plastic alongside their regular food. Then, we eat the shellfish whole, including the plastics still lodged in their systems. When will plastics become a regular part of autopsy reports? 86 percent of post-9/11 veterans who served in Iraq or Afghanistan say they were exposed to burn pits. Nobody counted how many civilians. Two years ago, on the anniversary of Powell's presentation, Azzawi extinguished the lights in the gallery that housed *Mission of Destruction* as a reference to the UN's decisions that day. He kept the lights off for 24 hours. "After Powell's speech, the military campaign was easy to win," Azzawi said. "The more difficult reality for the Iraqi people to face was the total destruction of their social and cultural infrastructure, which put an end to their daily life… Iraqis are dying every single day in the Land of Darkness." Actions speak louder than words. Do you agree? What is that spiralized razor wire called? Who invented it and why? Who makes it now? Chinese factory workers, Honduran, Egyptian, Alabamian: it matters who makes the things we use, even though we use them and then throw them in the trash. We bury almost everything without ceremony. I am afraid of too many things. Heights. Criticism. Some insects. The ocean. My own feelings. Scams. Sexual assault. Regrets. School shootings. Total ecological collapse. Death by methane. Death by plastic. The crumpled piece of paper next to me on the shiny blue bench: what do you think it says? On second glance, maybe it's just a wrapper. Writing poems on wrappers, napkins, bandages, soup labels, leaves, huge pieces of plastic sheeting, anything but paper. What would you write, and on what? Today, thinking is painful. Trash at the bus stop. Three paper coffee cups. Wendy's Hot & Crispy fries bag. Same, but McDonald's. Arizona iced tea. Tiny cranberry juice container. Plastic water bottle. Plastic lid. Plastic straw. Plastic clamshell takeout container. Plastic handle of an umbrella. All this plastic will outlast us, and we don't even know by how long.

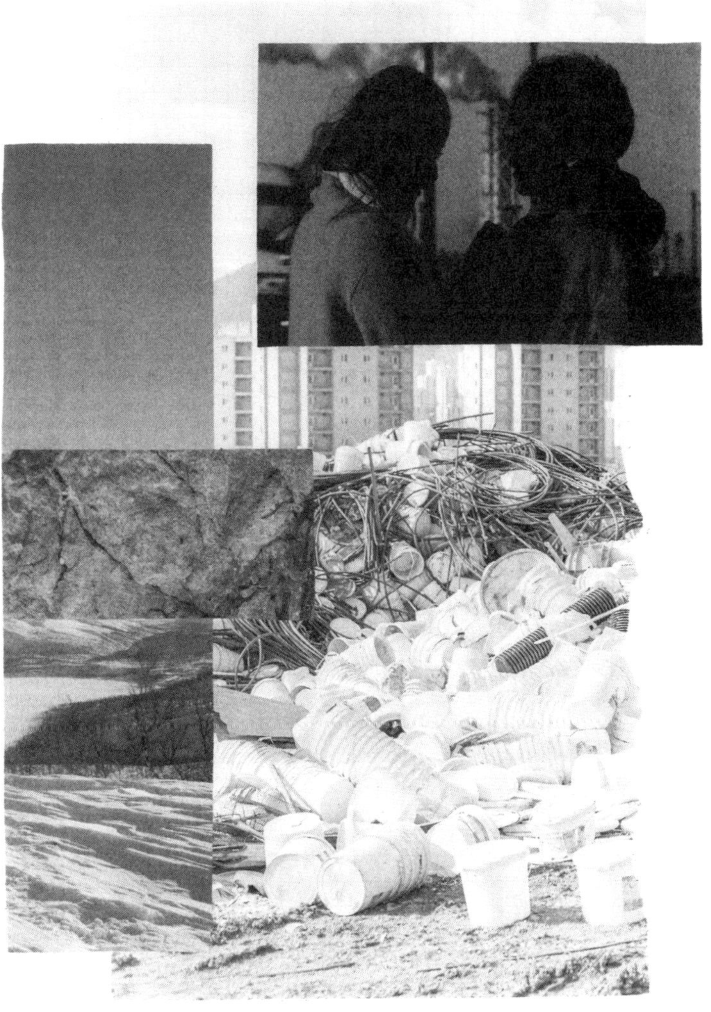

ACKNOWLEDGMENTS

I would like to thank Maggie Nelson for believing in this book and selecting it for publication. Her attention has meant the world to me, and she continues to be terrifically generous. I would also like to thank the Fonograf Editions team—Jeff Alessandrelli, Adie B. Steckel, and Ellena Basada—for shepherding this project into existence. In no particular order, the following people were also instrumental in this book's production: Torey Akers, Alexis Cheung, Becca Price, Emily Conner, Lynnsy Cobarrubia, Lana Lackey, Chaelee Dalton, Brielle Babiar, Brandi Kruse, Sarabeth Leitch, Matt Reed, Sarah Ashton, Alison Day, Trinity Toft, Leora Fuller, Mychal Denzel Smith, Saïd Sayrafiezadeh, Yami Vizcaino, Ingrid Dudek, Mom, Dad, Dylan Johnson, Kendra Gibbs, Alyssa Lewis, Melissa Aaker, Nicole Rizzo, Emily Kempf, Tyler Kohlhoff, John Torreano, Jessica Fenster-Sparber, Julia Kirkpatrick, Beth Lifson, Jamie Suehiro, the Creatives Rebuild New York grant, my students, my earliest mentor Linda Davis, and the writers Claudia Rankine, Hanif Abdurraqib, Olivia Liang, Cody Rose Clevidence, Dodie Bellamy, and of course Maggie Nelson, whose great work inspired the essays in this book. "Broken Crown" borrows from Abdurraqib's essay "Fear: A Crown," where I first encountered the sonnet crown form applied to an essay. "The Art of War" takes formal and thematic notes from Cody Rose Clevidence's book *Listen my Friend, This Is the Dream I Dreamed Last Night* and Dodie Bellamy's essay "July 4, 2011."

FONO
GRAF

1. **Eileen Myles**—*Aloha/irish trees* (LP)

2. **Rae Armantrout**—*Conflation* (LP)

3. **Alice Notley**—*Live in Seattle* (LP)

4. **Harmony Holiday**—*The Black Saint and the Sinnerman* (LP)

5. **Susan Howe & Nathaniel Mackey**—*STRAY: A Graphic Tone* (LP)

6. **Annelyse Gelman & Jason Grier**—*About Repulsion* (EP)

7. **Joshua Beckman**—*Some Mechanical Poems To Be Read Aloud* (print)

8. **Dao Strom**—*Instrument/ Traveler's Ode* (print; cassette tape)

9. **Douglas Kearney & Val Jeanty**—*Fodder* (LP)

10. **Mark Leidner**—*Returning the Sword to the Stone* (print)

11. **Charles Valle**—*Proof of Stake: An Elegy* (print)

12. **Emily Kendal Frey**—*LOVABILITY* (print)

13. **Brian Laidlaw and the Family Trade**—*THIS ASTER: adaptations of Emile Nelligan* (LP)

14. **Nathaniel Mackey and The Creaking Breeze Ensemble**—*Fugitive Equation* (compact disc)

15. *FE Magazine* (print)

16. **Brandi Katherine Herrera**—*MOTHER IS A BODY* (print)

17. J**an Verberkmoes**—*Firewatch* (print)

18. **Krystal Languell**—*Systems Thinking with Flowers* (print)

19. **Matvei Yankelevich**—*Dead Winter* (print)

20. **Cody-Rose Clevidence**—*Dearth & God's Green Mirth* (print)

21. **Hilary Plum**—*Hole Studies* (print)

22. **John Ashbery**—*Live at Sanders Theatre, 1976* (LP)

23. **Alice Notley**—*The Speak Angel Series* (print)

24. **Alice Notley**—*Early Works* (print)

25. **Joshua Marie Wilkinson**—*Trouble Finds You* (print)

26. **Timmy Straw**—*The Thomas Salto* (print)

27. **Audre Lorde**—*At Fassett Studio, 1970* (LP)

28. **Gabriel Palacios**—*A Ten Peso Burial For Which Truth I Sign* (print)

29. **Isabel Zapata, trans. Robin Myers**—*A Whale Is a Country* (print)

30. **Callum Angus**—*Cataract* (print)

31. *FE/De-Canon Anthology* (print)

32. **Cody-Rose Clevidence**—*The Grimace of Eden, Now* (print)

33. **Jaydra Johnson**—*Low: Notes on Art and Trash* (print)

34. **Jaime Gil de Biedma**—*If Only For a Moment (I'll Never Be Young Again)* (print)

Fonograf Editions is a registered 501(c)(3) nonprofit organization.
Find more information about the press at: fonografeditions.com.